INSPIRED BY QURAN

RECONNECT TO THE QURANIC LEGACY

AHMAD ABRAR

AURAQ

Printed in the Islamic Republic of Pakistan.
Printed: February, 2021
Edition: 1st
ISBN: 978-969-749-081-3
Price: Rs 1200 PKR, $12 US

ISLAMABAD, PAKISTAN

raabta@auraqpublications.com | +92-300-0571-530
www.auraqpublications.com | @AuraqPublications
ISBN : 978-969-749-081-3
Printed and Bound by *Passive Printers* - www.passiveprinters.com

DEDICATION

Dedicated to Al-Rahman, the Abundantly Loving, who guided us via Quran.

And Dedicated to the beautiful Parents and amazing Teachers and empowering Colleagues he has graced me with.

Thank you and JazakAllahukhayr to AbdulQadeer Greene, Tariq, Hakeem, Qawee, Ali and the whole Ramadan 2018 Quran class team who inspired the project, as well as to Dania who collected pages and supported the whole project, to Sheikha Asma AbdulHameed who reviewed it, to Muhammad Asif who beautifully transcribed the files, to Muhammad Usama my amazing friend and publisher of Auraq Publications for motivating me to polish and publish this work, and to all those mentioned and unmentioned who took part in this project. May Allah accept all those mentioned and those unmentioned with entry without accounting in the highest levels of Paradise with the company of the Prophet (S) and may Allah accept this work as a never-ending source of blessing for all humanity.

TABLE OF CONTENTS

INTRODUCTION

No book has had greater impact in world history and in the lives of mankind than the Quran. Through its revelations and through the Prophet Muhammad's ﷺ embodiment of it and his leadership, the Quran single-handedly revolutionized a backwards Arab people to become the spiritual and political leaders of the world.

For us believing Muslims this is not a surprising fact, given that we know and believe it to be the final and unaltered words of Allah, God, Himself sent to His final Prophet ﷺ.

The Quran is a living text. It was not just revealed as a set of idealistic principles, it was a play-by-play guidebook for the Messenger of Allah, Muhammad ﷺ.

What makes the Quran so special and what are its basic messages? How did the Prophet ﷺ live its instructions in order to become the spiritually grand and sublime character of a man that he became? How did he ﷺ, with the Quran's guidance, create the spiritual, religious, and political movement of Islam that has shaken the globe and continues to guide billions to this day? This and more is what this book attempts to explore. In exploring the Quran's teachings and how they guided the Prophet, we'll get a good introduction to the remarkable Quran and an appreciation of the way of life and the people and the great civilization and culture it created.

The Quran, being the Muslim constitution & the book of revealed spiritual guidance, has many facets to its messages, some of which are hard to decode at first. This is especially true for someone that picks it up without any context or prior knowledge and tries to read it as one does with any other book- from start to finish.

But when taken in the context that this was a revealed text sent to the Messenger of Allah ﷺ, the whole message becomes clearer and that much more powerful.

The Quran is truly what its name means, "the book that is oft-read." Oft-read why? Because people gain more and more healing and benefit and inspiration by reading it more and more. Serving true to its name, it is the most widely-memorized book on the planet and the book that is recited and chanted most often throughout the globe.

The story of Jesus is lost through the many different conflicting accounts found within the Bible that were compiled much after death. Yet, the story of Muhammad ﷺ is preserved by this divine revelation, one that was revealed during his lifetime and preserved by generations and generations of people that took it to memorization thereafter.

Even the Messenger of Allah ﷺ would pray, **"O Allah, I am Your slave, son of Your male servant, and son of Your** female servant. My forelock is in Your Hand. Your command for me prevails. Your judgement concerning me is just. I beseech You through every name You have, including those you have named Yourself, including that You have taught to anyone in Your creation, including those of your names that You have mentioned in Your Book, or that You have kept unknown that you make the Qur'an to be the Springtime of my heart, the light of my chest, the remover of my sadness and the pacifier of my worries. "** [Musnad Ahmad 1/391]*

What was he praying for? He was praying to Allah that may Allah make His words Quran such a guide and illuminator of my life that it is the springtime of my heart, constantly giving me spiritual abundance as is common in springtime to feed off of and live my spiritual life with.

And that's why after his ﷺ demise, his wife A'aishah R was asked what his ﷺ character was like. And she replied, *"His ﷺ character was the Quran."*

May Allah bless you and I to also be included amongst such honoured people who learn to appreciate and illuminate their spirits and their lives by virtue of the Divine words. May we become amongst those truly inspired by Quran. Ameen.

HOW THIS BOOK IS ORGANIZED

The Quran is too vast to cover all of its subjects in a short volume like this one. So what have we done to go into the crux of its messages? We've broken it down into 3 primary subjects that we will focus on: 1) "The Direction" section (Foundational stories and beliefs and mindsets that the Quran gives us), 2) "The Practice" section (the spiritual practices and rituals and ethical rules of being a Muslim that the Quran guides us towards), and 3) "The Mission" Section (establishing a strong community and being containers of light and love and guidance spreading the beauty of Islam across the globe).

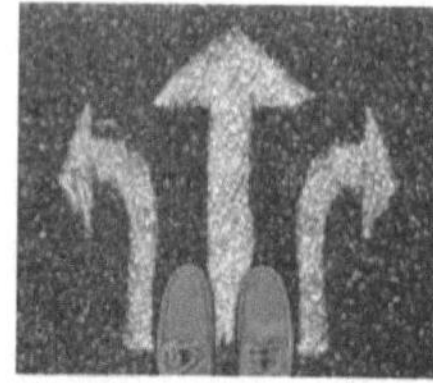

In "The Direction" section, we will first look at the beliefs and mindset that the Quran inculcated in the Prophet ﷺ and his followers. This displays the beliefs that we too need to ground in our hearts and displays Prophet's ﷺ role as the firmest of all believers in the Truth revealed to him ﷺ.

From there, we'll then go into "The Practice" section, the guidelines for individual spirituality and religious practice that the Quran and that Islam establishes. This will display the Prophet's ﷺ role as a righteous man that lived with strong ethical principles and a spiritual giant.

Lastly, we'll go over the guidelines of how the Quran guided the community of Muslims and its spread across the globe. This will display the Prophet's ﷺ role as a missionary and caller to Allah and His Way. We will also then discuss how the Quran emphasizes in us also establishing a strong community and being containers of light and love and guidance spreading the beauty of Islam across the globe like the Prophet ﷺ and his companions did. All three are his primary roles as the final Messenger of Allah ﷺ that we too need to learn about, emulate him in, and make our own. We pray that we all become people whose character is the Quran and who become firm believers, righteous servants of Allah, and passionate missionaries working hard for the betterment and guidance of our local and global communities.

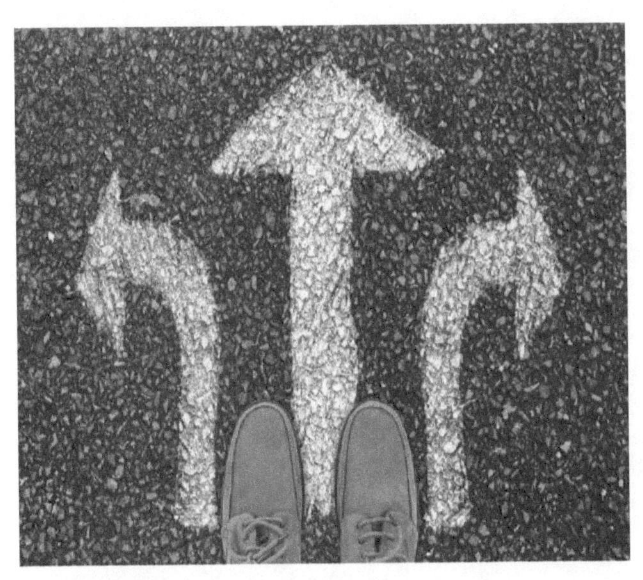

SECTION 1:

DIRECTION

APPRECIATING THE ART OF CREATION (& THE CREATOR BEHIND IT ALL)

Walk with me as we stare in awe of the starry night sky of the desert. Get lost in the sky and the thousands of glimmering stars out in the distance. Where are you? On a floating tiny spec amongst the vast cosmos. "There must be an All-Knowing designer behind it all!" That is what the natural primordial heart embraced in nature always concludes.

The Prophet ﷺ loved nature, respected it, and was spiritually one with it. Time in nature was something he was fond of since his upbringing, and the Quran and his spiritual growth in coming nearer to Allah enhanced his relation to it that much more.

When Allah mentions the beauty of creation and of His art how magnificently the natural world is running by His hands, He calls such phenomena an "ayah." What's an ayah? It's a miraculous proof and sign and pointer of His existence and His glory. Ayahs are phenomena in our human experience that are self-evident pointers to His existence and glory. Ayahs are messages reminding the heart that Allah is great, Allah is present, Allah is running the whole show. When you truly experience an ayah you gain a deeper sense of awe and recognition of the Creator and Director behind it all. The Ayahs are all around us. And the Prophet ﷺ as well as the true believers that follow him can see them clearly so they live a life of awe.

> *"Verily in the creation of the heavens and the earth and in the succession of the might and the day, and in the ships that sped through the sea for what is useful to man, and in the waters that Allah sends down from the sky, giving life to the earth after it had been lifeless and in living creatures multiplying thereon, and in the change of the winds, and in the clouds that run their appointed courses between the sky and earth are clear signs (ayahs) for people who understand."*

(Quran 2:164)

What is Allah telling us here? Here Allah is telling us that He's given us sign after sign and message after message in the daily wonders of nature and in our experience and life advancement that point to Allah as a conscious creative power illuminating and running the universe in harmony and beauty. Life is bubbling and bustling all over, speaking its message pointing at Allah's Oneness.

> *"All that is in the heavens and on the earth extol Allah's limitless glory for He alone is Almighty and truly wise."*

(Quran 57:1)

Here Allah is telling us, as a sign of further glorification for His greatness, that not only are those natural wonders pointing to the magnificence of their Creator, they inherently and in the deeper realm (that most of us can't perceive) constantly and continuously sing and extol Allah's glory! That the whole heavens and earth is a big chorus of divine praise. And yet the eyes return towards us. All of creation recognize Allah's glory, so then how come you, oh man, claiming so much intelligence for yourself, can't recognize and celebrate such praises and live in obedience to that one and only Creator? What's holding you back from living purely in obedience to the One who created you?

"Would it be reasonable if I did not serve Him Who created me, and to Whom all of you shall be brought back?"

(Quran 36:22)

"O man! What has seduced you from your Lord Most Beneficent? The One who created you, proportioned you, and fashioned you in balance; In whatever Form He wills, does He put you together."

(Quran 82:6-8)

Nature and revelation have complementary roles in our lives as believers. For it is in the context of us being a part of the natural world that Allah created that we experience the world, and it is through the word that Allah spoke, and revealed that we learn how to see the world and live in natural harmony in it. Both The Word (the Quran) and The World (nature) point to the Greatness of Him and His nearness to us.

What are some of the key lessons we learn from through nature? One of the key lessons of nature is symmetry and beauty that is present all over our physical dimension by Divine Design, a glimpse of reflection in the greater perfections of the higher realms. It reminds the believer of the realm of Paradise that He praises so much must be that much more perfect and beautiful. It is reminder of perfection for us, a perfection that we innately seek. Another lesson is the cycle of life and how things live to their prime and then wither and die, expressing the fleeting nature of time for all of us. Things are always moving forward and soon it will be our time to move onward from this life to the next. This awareness gives those who reflect and truly understand this principle a deeper purpose to life, for everything in existence is doing what it was created to do yet the question is, "Are we doing what we were created to do?" In due our time on earthly existence will cease, and our future existence will be either one of eternal joy or of never-ending pain based on whether we passed this test of life and worldly existence or not.

Listen to these powerful verses:

"To Allah belongs the dominion of the heavens and the earth; and Allah has power over all things. Behold! in the creation of the heavens and the earth, and in the alternation of night and day, are indeed Signs for men of understanding! Men who celebrate the praises of Allah, standing, sitting, and lying down on their sides, and (men who) while contemplating the (wonders and design of) creation in the heavens and the earth (exclaim):

'Our Lord! You did not create all this in vain! Glorified are You! Give us salvation from the penalty of the Fire. Our Lord! Any whom You do admit to the Fire, Truly you cover with shame, and never will wrong-doers Find any helpers! Our Lord! we have heard the call of one calling (Us) to Faith, 'Believe you in the Lord,' and we have believed. Our Lord! Forgive us our sins, blot out from us our iniquities, and take to Thyself our souls in the company of the righteous. Our Lord! Grant us what you did promise to us through Your Prophets, and save us from

shame on the Day of Judgment: for You are One who never breaks Your promise.'

And their Lord accepted of them and answered them: 'Never will I suffer to be lost the work of any of you, be he male or female: You are members, one of another: Those who have left their homes, or been driven out therefrom, or suffered harm in My Cause, or fought or have been slain: Verily, I will blot out from them their sins, and admit them into Gardens with rivers flowing beneath! A reward from the presence of Allah, and from His presence is the best of rewards."

(Quran 3:189-195)

From this passage, we understand that the men who are truly understanding of reality are those who appreciate nature and who realize the Creator behind it all. They know they were made in this existence for a purpose. And because of their understanding and their living righteously, Allah answers their prayers and makes them amongst the successful of Paradise, a reality whose beauty and joy is far beyond that of this realm!

Nature develops in us a sense of wonder and awe. When we stare at the starry night, one can't help but be awestruck by the vastness of the Universe and the mystery of the sight and the stars and the cosmos and beyond. What actually lies beyond our senses? What intelligence has created such a beautiful starry experience of the night for us? What does that intelligence, the Intelligence of the All-Knowing, have written and planned for us beyond our earthly existences? Let this mystery fascinate and envelope your conscience.

The starry night awakens the innate human desire to receive messages from what is far out and beyond us, and the Quran is indeed the message that we so deeply and innately seek, a revelation sent from above and beyond us, from the Creator behind it all! The true believer gets a sense of awe looking at the magnificence of creation, and for the believer it is a similar enrapturing of awe we experience listening to the magnificence of the Divine speech. The heart moves without thinking & fills with love and awe realizing this is Allah's mercy sent down to us, that this Quran is Allah directly communicating with us! This very Book is our essential guide to understanding our place and role in the cosmos. And that is why those who truly understand it and live it, following the example of the Messenger of the Quran ﷺ, spend hours reciting revelation under the starry night and in the early hours of dawn. And in the day time they reflect the light they have gathered alone by living as shining examples of the beautiful guidelines and life example set via the Quran and the Messenger of Allah ﷺ. Another lesson we learn from the Quran as we live in this natural world is humility. The vastness of the oceans and the desert also bring about humility and vulnerability for how little we are compared to their vastness and how easily we can be swallowed by them to fade away into nothingness! Our earthly forms live by the motto: from earth we were made and to it we shall return! Whereas our spirit and higher consciousness makes us transcend to the higher truth: To Allah we belong and to Him we shall return! All the movements in the heavens and the lands and oceans and even the movements in the universe of our lives all call towards our return back to Him and our desperate need of His Grace.

The vastness of the cosmos is mind-boggling. We now believe that this universe that we see was started around 13.78 billion light years ago and has a diameter of around 100 billion light years and has around 200 billion galaxies according to our best scientific research so far! This big earth makes for a tiny floating planet in the solar system, and compared to the vast Milky Way Galaxy that we are in we are just an invisible spec! And the Prophet ﷺ also mentioned a multiverse setup that Allah has created such that this universe that we are researching or "first sky" as it is referred to in the Quran is only one dimension of our immediate experience, and that there are six more universes on top of it, being so vast that they are beyond our comprehension!

We live in a time where a lot of the natural world on earth is in danger because of our own human hands. In our Islamic tradition, we understand that the natural world is in more chaos not only because we are directly harming it but also because our collective spiritual world is in more chaos. Thus, although scientific solutions and efforts that help like ways to reduce pollution and recycle more must not be abandoned, it can never be enough if our spiritual health and order is ignored. Humanity must learn to pray like the Prophet ﷺ prayed and to be a detached minimalist when it comes to the world and consumption within it. Humanity, by and large, has been fooled into the snares of extreme materialism, living for this life in the world and living for the most pleasure and most accumulation of experiences, love, wealth, power, and resources that we can have. As a human race, we worship our own desires and their commands over Allah and His commands, we live for this life at the expense of our afterlife, we live in misguidance at the expense of guidance, and we work and toil for our own immediate pleasure and benefit without realizing that we are actually leading ourselves to our own eternal destruction. Living in the Islamic and Prophetic manner is the heart of restoring our hearts, our lives, and our natural world back to harmony.

KEEPING IT REAL

Now it's Your Turn:

1. Go out for 10 minutes a day for a walk or just sitting outside and reflecting on Allah's wondrous creation and the All-Knowing and All-Creating behind it all.

2. Try reciting Quran while out in nature and try to feel a deeper connection with the words of your Creator.

3. Memorize the Quranic prayer, "*Our Lord! You did not create all this in vain! Glorified are You! Give us salvation from the penalty of the Fire.*"

Reflection Questions:

1. How much time am I giving daily to disconnect from the world and simply to reflect in nature?

2. Why did Allah create such diversity and beauty and symmetry in nature?

3. Why is nature always a subject oft-repeated by Allah in the Quran? Where does it lead the human being towards?

THE GREAT MEETING

One of the most significant events in human history was the meeting of Allah with Musa AS. Through it, Allah teaches the Prophet ﷺ and all of us the Great yet also loving and caring Lord that He is and the reality of the test of life that He has set up.

Let's go over verses 6-16 of the 20th chapter of the Quran (known as Surah Taha) which powerfully and briefly captures the lofty event:

> *To Him belongs what is in the heavens and on the earth, and all between them, and all that is beneath the soil. If you pronounce the word aloud (or not, it is no matter:) for verily He knows what is secret and what is yet more hidden. Allah, there is no god but He! To Him belong the most Beautiful Names.*
>
> *Has the story of Moses reached you? When he saw a fire and said to his family, 'Stay here; indeed, I have perceived a fire; perhaps I can bring you a torch or find at the fire some guidance.'*

But when he came to the fire, a voice was heard: 'O Musa! Verily I am Your Lord! Therefore (in My presence) put off Your shoes: you are in the sacred valley Tuwa. I have chosen You: listen, then, to the inspiration (sent to you). Verily, I am Allah, There is no god but I: So serve Me (only), and establish regular prayer for celebrating My praise. Verily the Hour is coming, (and) My design (of life) is to keep it hidden (until the right time), so that every soul shall receive its reward by the measure of their endeavour. Therefore let not those who don't believe but rather follow their own lusts divert you from this lest you perish!'"

(Quran 20: 6-16)

These above verses start by a praises of Allah then come down to the human dimension of us interacting with Him.

Has the story of Musa reached you? When he saw a fire and said to his family, 'Stay here; indeed, I have perceived a fire; perhaps I can bring you a torch or find at the fire some guidance.'

Allah starts by painting for us a scene of Musa (AS) being lost with his family in the Sinai desert and then suddenly seeing a fire atop one of the mountains. He tells his family that he'll go hike up there alone to get some fire or some direction for them.

Musa AS was basically telling his family to wait there while he goes up and gets some guidance in terms of perhaps finding locals there that could point him to the right physical direction to safe staying and their intended destination. Oh what a surprise he was in for! For he didn't realize the guidance he was about to receive was the greatest of guidance, from the Ultimate Creator and Guide Himself, as he would be atop that mount.

Allah continues and says:

"But when he came to the fire, a voice was heard: 'O Musa! Verily I am thy Lord! Therefore (in My presence) put off thy shoes: You are in the sacred valley Tuwa. I have chosen you: listen, then, to the inspiration (sent to you).'"

Musa AS had loved Allah and served him devotionally and interacted with Him throughout his life like a faithful believer does. Yet although he knew and believed Allah saw him and heard him, he like the other true believers of the time, was awaiting death and then the Great Meeting after that to finally meet and hear from His beloved Lord.

Though for this specific servant of His, Allah had very different plans. Miraculously, and out of the love and generosity to Musa AS, Allah spoke to him directly, in a manner and with a way of revelation that we cannot grasp. Musa AS was in awe and completely humbled, it was His beloved Lord He was now in the presence of giving Him direct attention.

Take off your shoes Musa AS! And come humbly! For now you are about to receive the guidance by Allah Himself! And He always reveals with complete knowledge and from the realms of the Unperceivable reality as to direct our lives in the most holy and most beautiful of fashions!

Now let's move forward. What was the essential revelation that Allah wanted Musa AS to listen carefully to?

THE KEY MESSAGES ALLAH GIVES TO MUSA (AS)

Let's all listen up and pay attention to what Allah says to Him:

"Verily, I am Allah. There is no god but I: So serve you Me (only), and establish regular prayer for celebrating My praise. Verily the Hour is coming, (and) My design (of life)

is to keep it hidden (until the right time), for every soul to receive its reward by the measure of its endeavour. Therefore let not those who don't believe but rather follow their own lusts divert you from this lest you perish!"

(Quran 20: 14-16)

Imagine the fascination the Prophet ﷺ had when he first heard these verses. Here was his fellow Prophet, Musa AS, that had come years ago and yet He is meeting Allah for the first time directly. And what did Allah tell him? The same messaages of Oneness and preparation for the Last Day like Allah was revealing to Muhammad ﷺ! This stories served as a way to build the identity and confidence of the Prophet ﷺ and the companions. Regardless of the odds and the resistance you face, you are on the right side of history, Oh Muslims!

Every Friday, we Muslims go to Jumu'ah Friday service to hear a sermon to remind ourselves of Allah, His Prophet ﷺ, and the Last Day. But in this great historic event for humanity, it is not man that is preaching, but rather it is Allah, the Almighty Himself, giving His sermon to His chosen servant, Musa AS! Imagine how profound and how much greater that meeting was compared to any other!

So what did Allah first say to him in these above verses? There are four main subjects that Allah addressed, subjects that are the essence of Islam as well.

Firstly, Allah proclaims His Oneness and that Musa AS has been on the right path for serving and worshipping Allah alone. Allah is the Only One worthy of worship, the only divinity, and He always was so and always will be so. This also is the first commandment that was given to Musa AS and is the heart of the shahadah, the testimony of faith, that one must believe in and proclaim in order to become a Muslim and be amongst the saved.

Secondly, Allah commands him to establish the Salah (ritual prayer) filled with His remembrance. Allah doesn't say, "go pray," He says, "Stand firmly to establish the prayer" to Musa (AS) as a command to him and a reminder to the rest of us that are now being narrated the fateful events of that blessed encounter. What is the wisdom of saying establish the prayer instead of just commanding one to prayer? And how come Allah always uses this wording in the Quran when commanding us to pray throughout the Quran?

Malcolm X said it best when he said, "A man who stands for nothing will fall for anything." Meaning when a man stands for justice or truth or beauty or something that he believes in, then he doesn't fall into the pressures of society and the distractions around him. And by Allah saying, "Stand firmly to establish the prayer," He is saying that He is the only One in essence worthy of believing in and stand for and by doing so you will be successful and won't fall for the distractions traps set around you! What beauty there is in Allah's wordings! This is the gift of this ritual prayer of salah that Allah has blessed us and it is so important that you must commit to establish it in your life, and revolve the rest of your life around it!

This also shows us that salah, the ritual prayer that we as Muslims do that includes standing, bowing, and prostrating, is not a new ritual that was given exclusively to the Prophet Muhammad ﷺ, but rather is a historically established ritual that has been practiced for centuries, including being a practice for Musa AS and the Jews who originally followed him and for Jesus AS and for the men that originally followed him. On a more deeper level, knowing that current Jews and Christians don't pray salah and have only scarce remnants of prayer rituals if any left is a reminder that if we do not stay firm then we will lose our gifts and be amongst the misguided like previous communities are, and that only by surrendering our will to Allah can we be amongst the true Muslims who have one of the great honors and good fortunes of being the only community that has kept the salah and the right way to worship Allah alive and well today.

In my journey to call people to Islam, I have met Christians that have said statements like, "How come you guys pray like that to God in set movements and at set times? We pray to God and have such a connection that we can pray to Him at anytime and anywhere, all we have to do is call on Him." To which the simple reply was, "We too can call on God and speak to Him anytime and anywhere on our own time, but we also honor God by doing the ritual prayers that He commanded us to do at specific times in a way and manner that He loves. It is a ritual prayer that Moses and Jesus and his true followers also were also commanded to do and did but that you who claim to follow him in today's time have all but forgotten by now!" The orthodox Jews usually never ask as they understand, and also admit that they do a prostration once a year and used to do a bowing that they have lost since. How far the Jews and Christians have gone from the pure sacred teachings of their prophets! Allah protect us from such a foul end!

The last part of the command is also important which is that Allah adds a descriptor to what prayer and salah should be all about. He says, "Establish the prayer <u>in my remembrance</u>." That the purpose of prayer is not just to do certain postures like some may even do while practicing yoga as to open certain chakras (spiritual energy centers within the body), which may even be side benefits of the prayer, the ultimate purpose of the prayer is to remember Allah and celebrate His praises in loving and in beautiful devotion.

Developing the right heart before the Lord, one that is in love with Him and is in constant remembrance of Him, is just as important as learning the right postures and timings and proper way of purifying ourselves for the salah prayer. Thus the salah is the perfect merging of both the physical realm and the spiritual, the perfect contemplative and meditative experience that opens the door to deeper discovery of self and deeper discovery of the glory of our Lord. This is why it's a practice Allah has prescribed throughout the ages for the Believers: within the simplicity of the movements and sacred mantra incantations of the divine words are hidden spiritual secrets and powers awaiting the righteous and the truly devoted to experience.

The third thing that Allah brings up to Musa AS is the big-picture reality of life, that there is an enormous and epic Day of Judgement coming, a Day that Allah has kept hidden, and that it will ultimately be the day people are repaid for the beliefs and lives that they have lived. Life's whole purpose was to serve Allah and obey Him fully and if one does so and one had pure beliefs and a pure life, then such a good karma life and such a good energy of life will be well-appreciated and accepted by the Most High! For such souls is the ultimate home, where eternal bliss is promised in the gracious dwellings of the gardens of Paradise known as Jannah, and the ultimate company, of Allah and His Messenger and all the accepted righteous men and women themselves!

Yet as for those who lived based on the lies that they were told, lies that were contrary to the blessed revelation, and yet continued to believe in falsehood and live wretchedly, for them they will be repaid in full for their falling off the path, and the recompense of such is nothing short of Hell, the blazing and despair-giving fire pit of an abode that leaves no one that enters it, what a terrible dwelling it is! Thus the wise revolve their life around Allah and His revelation and the day they will ultimately meet Him, begging and hoping for redemption and forgiveness and His acceptance so they may gain the Gardens and His eternal love, and fearful and scared of His disappointment and anger and being humiliated and thrown into the Fire.

The last command Allah mentioned in these verses is a command to stay away from one of the greatest threats to our faith and our relationship to Allah and our final outcome. What could be such a great threat such that Allah is even commanding Musa AS to stand guard from it? Bad company!

Allah is telling Musa AS and reminding all of us to guard and stay as best away from those that deter us and derail us from the path. This means staying as best away from those that don't believe in Allah or live accordingly, to stay away from those who live a lifestyle against the teachings of Allah and His Prophet S and who pull you down in with them. This does not mean you do not interact with any unrighteous or nonbelieving individuals at all, for many a times it is a necessity especially when in minority Muslim countries, but it does mean that if you get close enough to them and they get close enough to you that they start influencing you in the wrong direction, it could mean your destruction, so stay wary!

Their influence will divert us and will weaken our heart's faith and slowly but surely if we are not careful then the tower of faith we built will crumble and we may soon find ourselves to be amongst the misguided and perished and destroyed, Allah protect us! The verse clarifies the 2 qualities of this distracting group of people that will make you stray. First off, they don't really believe, and their lifestyle and choices show it. And secondly they follow their own desires. You believe in Allah and follow revelation, they believe in themselves and alternatives and follow their own conjecture and desires. You are different. Don't ever fall for them or let them divert you from the truth that you have been given.

In summary, Allah tells Musa AS and is telling all of us the same advice of believing in Him and living for the Last Day when we meet Him and will be accounted and that we should revolve our lives around ritual prayer with His remembrance and we should always shun those people and those social situations and those groups that by us involving ourselves in will distract and divert us from the path of love and worship and obedience.

HE WAS ALWAYS THERE

What I love about Surah Taha is that as authoritarian and awe-commanding Allah is (And He deserves to be as He is the Almighty Himself!) and displays Himself in his interaction with Musa AS, yet still He, with His profound and eternal wisdom and bountiful care for His creation, isn't shy to express His love to Musa AS.

In verses 36-41, Allah grants Musa AS his requests that he asks for, and then says a few statements that touches my heart each time I hear the sweet words He express to Musa. Life for a lot of us unfolds and happens in unexpected ways and especially when tragedy happens life doesn't make sense for a lot of us. Why would Allah do this to me? The unique part of our relationship to Allah is that we speak to Him and believe in Him and He hears us yet we don't yet hear Him directly. We wait for the Day where we will meet Him, where He will connect all the dots of our life, and hopefully lovingly and generously forgive us and accept us in His eternal grace. Musa AS was no different. He was born in a tough political climate as a Jewish minority in Egyptian lands, was raised in the hands of his people's enemy, and happened to accidentally kill a man in his prime that led to public humiliation and exile. It was painful and even though Musa AS had since moved on, there was that lingering feeling of why it all happened.

And now here Musa AS is with Allah, speaking to Him directly and being assigned a great missionary task. And so Allah so lovingly reminds Musa AS that He was there the whole time and has a special love for Musa AS. I cannot imagine the depth of the melting of his heart and the stream of tears that ran through Musa's AS face as he heard these words:

(Allah) said: "Granted is your prayer, O Musa!" And indeed We conferred a favour on you another time (before). "Behold! We sent to thy mother, by inspiration, the message: "Throw (the child) into the chest, and throw (the chest) into the river: the river will cast him up on the bank, and he will be taken up by one who is an enemy to Me and an enemy to him': But I cast (the garment of) love over you from Me: and (this) in order that you mayest be reared under Mine eye. "Behold! Thy sister goeth forth and saith, 'shall I show you one who will nurse and rear the (child)?' So We brought you back to thy mother, that her eye might be cooled and she should not grieve. Then you didst slay a man, but We saved you from trouble, and We tried you in various ways. Then didst you tarry a number

of years with the people of Midian. Then didst you come hither as ordained, O Moses! "And I have prepared you for Myself (for service).

Allah out of love recounts Musa's AS life for Him, as a way to let him know that Allah was there watching him and having his back the whole time. It's as if it is Allah is telling him, "Musa! Even when you weren't old enough to comprehend, I was there. From the time of your birth to the moment of your manhood and to this point, I was there. Just like it was my Decree that led you to be nurtured by your very enemy, so too was it my Decree and Destiny that you would kill that man, and that now after so many years you would meet me. Yes I loved you and supported you and was present throughout all your life, even those moments you weren't aware of, even those moments where life was hard and it wasn't so self-evident."

My favorite two parts are how Allah gives insight into the deepest why behind the life events by saying

1)　　"But I cast (the garment of) love over you from Me: and (this) in order that you may be raised under My eye…."

2)　　"Then did you come here as ordained, O Musa! And I have prepared you for Myself (for His special love and for His service)"

The first statement was said after Allah reminded Musa AS that he was raised in the house of the enemy of his people! How else could that be possible except from the mercy of Allah! And so Allah says so lovingly, "I cast My Love over you and did all this so you could be raised under my eye."

The second statement was said after Allah mentioned the struggle that first his mother and his sister went through when they left Musa AS in the cradle and how Allah blessed them in a unique way to stay connected to Musa AS and then Allah mentioned different struggles that Musa AS had to go through. What was all that struggle for? It was part of the relationship Allah had with Musa AS, Allah gave him challenges too so that He may grow. This is why Allah keeps repeating the fact that He actually did the things, He reunited his mother with him, He tested Him, He ordained that this meeting happen. "Then did you come here as ordained, O Musa! And I have prepared you for Myself (for service)." This statement ends in a way that sums up struggle for us all if we are sincere: Allah has ordained our struggles in order that we may be purified and be accepted in His total service.

If we have faith, the good in our life is because of His love and grace on us, and the struggles are there as what is pre-ordained by Allah and all of it is so we can be made pure and be admitted into pure service for Him. What an honor it is to be selected for Him!

Here is Musa AS who accidentally killed a man, who was known as a murderer throughout the Egyptian lands, whose own Jewish community disowned him, whose own Egyptian community wanted him killed and had him on the most wanted list.

People considered him out but Allah did not. Indeed in Allah's eyes he was worthy of love, was purified and was chosen for great things by the Almighty Himself! Musa AS even considered himself out of Egyptian life and had for so long lived remotely from there. Yet his simply pure faithful life was a training till he was ready and till Allah's decree manifested for

Musa AS to do higher-assigned tasks and greater things for Allah's sake. Allah knew his heart, forgave him for his past, and cast His own love on Him such that He was chosen directly by Allah Himself!

We all too have our own past whether that be the little sins or big ones. But don't consider any past too big for Allah to forgive. Turn to Allah, go more slowly and faithfully and righteously and always choose good righteous company, and if Allah wills He shall honor us and raise us high among the righteous like He so generously did with Musa AS!

TRANSCENDENT YET SO LOVING

Look at the vastness of space, the innumerable stars, the enormous galaxies, the asteroids, the planets, the supernovas, the black holes, and everything else in between and you will be in awe of the transcendent One behind it all. We are such a little insignificant part of existence, we really are. Have you seen the earth's size in comparison to the sun? To the Galaxy? To other bigger stars? We are not even a spec in many galactic maps!

Yet here is a Lord we are interacting with that is literally behind it ALL! The Creator and sustainer of all existences. Whatever you conceive of, He is far greater! And that he loves us and has chosen Us for His service.

To Allah, even the existences that to us are so big, are nothing. To Allah the whole universe is nothing in comparison to Him. He says Be and it is and there is no hardship He faces in such manifesting of existence.

What I am getting at and this is an obvious fact for the intelligent who reflect is that Allah is so transcendent that He doesn't have to care for us at all. He doesn't have to be so generous in offering us an eternal ticket for Paradise for faith and righteousness, nor does He have to look after the world or people in it and creating the balance in it that expresses the most eternal benefit for those who seek Him. We are such small existences in such a vast network of multi-dimensional existences, both of those we know and those we don't know! He didn't have to. In fact, if Allah wanted, He didn't even have to create us at all! So why did He even create us? Why the test of our existence towards righteousness? Because he loves those lovers who live to please Him so He did all this. Yes, this creation of humanity and our whole life existence is all just a test of love. And if we live it right it will be a story of love where the mutual lovers will reunite with their beloveds (Allah with us and us with Allah).

He cares for us out of love for us, He guides us out of love for us, and He forgives us out of His forbearing and merciful nature and disposition towards us. It wouldn't add to Allah's kingdom or to His greatness even if all of us were the most righteous, for He is in no need of us and we are in complete need of Him. His call for our righteousness and loyalty and obedience is for our own good and for our own long-term benefit; none of our deeds He needs, for it is all just a test from Him so He sees who really loves Him and is loyal to Him and who rejects and disobeys Him.

Right after the powerful verse of the chair that we reviewed earlier, Allah lovingly calls us to holding on to Him and befriending Him through firm faith and trust in Him:

> *"[Even though Allah is so incomparably above all else that you would totally obey Him if you knew His grand position, still] let there be no compulsion in religion. The*

sensible path has been clarified from the nonsensical one. So whoever denies the false others and believes and trusts in Allah (alone), then he has grasped a strong handhold- one that will never break! And Allah is the All-Hearing, the All-Knowing. Allah is the protector and friend of those who trust in Him, He pulls them out from the darknesses into The Light. As for those who deny, they make their protectors the false and rebellious others. Those false others pull them away from The Light and into the darknesses. These are the dwellers of the Fire, in it they shall dwell in forever!"

(Quran 2:256-257)

Allah is Gentle so he doesn't force anyone to follow His guidance but lets people make their choice to either obey or disobey, to follow or to not follow, on their own. Thus they will be rewarded or punished accordingly in the next life.

He teaches and reveals it as to guide us to the right way. He is ready to "hold our hand" meaning ready to help us and pulls into the right way of living that will lead to ultimate illumination and success. He is ready to take us along straight into His eternal beloved company in Jannah [Paradise], if we are ready to take Him up on His offer. And He is the All-Hearing and All-Knowing, hearing our voices and the voices of our heart and supporting us when we are struggling. He is here for us and knows everything about us. He cares for us. As long as we put our trust in Him with full sincerity and loyalty, He will be our friend and protector pulling us into higher realms of illumination for us to transcend ourselves and our current physical selves. He's the One for us to trust and put all our marbles in and our bets on.

And not only is Allah able to listen to us, but also He is so loving that He LOVES listening to us! He says Himself:

"When My servants ask you concerning Me, I am indeed close (to them): I listen to the prayer of every supplicant when he calls on Me: Let them also, with a will, Listen to My call, and believe in Me: That they may walk in the right way."

(Quran 2:186)

In the world, usually the higher in rank a person is, the harder he is to reach. And the lower a person is in rank in the world, the less access he has to those higher. Yet here is Allah, the greatest of all the greatest, the One with no comparison in superiority, telling us, the lowly servants with no status and no standing, who are but a small dust particle on a floating dust particle called the Earth, and He in all of His glory is telling us that when we call on Him He is near and listening! Indeed this is nothing but love, so let those who are seeking Him reflect on His generosity!

Calling on Him goes double so when it is His forgiveness and Paradise it is we are asking for.

"And those who commit an indecency or wrong themselves and (immediately thereafter) remember Allah then seek forgiveness for their sins. And who else can forgive except for Allah?"

(Quran 3:135)

Even when you mess up and sin or when you have sinned who else is there to turn to other than Your Creator, the One who is forbearing with you, the One ready to forgive the sincerely repentant, the One and Only Allah?

*"Rush towards forgiveness from Your Lord and Gardens
(of Paradise) that are as wide as the heavens and the earth,
(a reward) prepared for the righteous!"*

(Quran 3:133)

It's beautiful how here Allah calls us to rush towards His forgiveness and then towards such a vast kingdom of Paradise filled with Gardens, connotating that even if we've messed up in life if we straighten ourselves and live purely and righteously for Him we can gain full redemption and be amongst the eternally successful. May we be blessed to be amongst such, Ameen!

KEEPING IT REAL

Now it's Your Turn:

1. Go out today and look for moments where you can "find Allah," meaning where you can get aware of His presence with you and watch over you.

2. Allah told even the great Musa AS to keep and maintain his prayers, so we have no excuses and have to do the same! How many of the obligatory 5 prayers are you praying on time? Make a schedule and a goal to do them all!

3. Company is a powerful driver of either positive or negative change which is why Allah told Musa AS to stay wary of those who could lead him to destruction. Who are your friends? Are they empowering you to come closer to Allah or not? The people that are in your life, befriend! And those who are pulling you away from Allah, from them you should run away!

Reflection Questions:

1. What are things you are struggling with now that may be divine blessings guiding you towards Him just like Musa AS was guided towards purification and prophethood after his accidental killing of a man?

2. *"When My servants ask you concerning Me, I am indeed close (to them)!"*

What are things you desperately want in life? What are things you should start asking for and with deeper desperation? Which time will you set out everyday to do at least some imploring on Allah and calling on Him?

3. How big of a day will the day of Judgement be? Why did Allah keep it hidden? How will Allah reward/punish each person for their deeds?

THE GREAT REINCARNATION

For those of other traditions that then came to the beautiful folds of the Islamic faith, the clarity the Quran expresses in terms of the events of the afterlife is mesmerizing. With just as much force as the truth of God's oneness and of the sanctity and true life stories of the prophets does the Quran establish the realities of the Day of Judgement and heaven and hell that are soon coming. It leaves no doubt in the sincere reader's heart that there is indeed a Big Day of Accounting soon coming. And that those who did not embrace the way of Islam and the way of the Prophets will be doomed and taste destruction and regret like they have never experienced ever before.

THE GREAT ACCOUNTING

The Quran came as a glad tiding to the believers who believe in and follow Muhammad ﷺ and as a stern warning to those who turn away and rejection. A warning from what? From a Great Day where all their denial in Allah's oneness, their rejecting of Islam, and all of their evil actions will be accounted for in total.

The Quran came to clarify such key metaphysical issues like what will happen to us after our death and how the unseen realm functions that many people of different faiths and philosophies have different views about. Allah speaks about these realities with such force and such details leaving no doubt in the believers' hearts on how things work behind the scenes and what will happen to all of us when we die.

The Pagan Arabs around the Prophet ﷺ had a concept of a creator and life force that initiated the universe yet they are similar in beliefs to modern secular atheists and in any possible existence of an afterlife. You only live once is the motto many live by unfortunately.

A disbelieving man came to the Prophet ﷺ and rudely took some dry decomposed animal bones (like that of chicken) and threw it in front of the Prophet and mockingly said: "Who can give life to these dry bones, decomposed and lifeless?"

Allah replied directly to his challenge through Quran revelation:

> *"Let not their speech grieve you. Certainly we know what they hide alongside whatever they may disclose.*
>
> *Does not man see that it is We Who created him from sperm? Yet behold! He strands forth as an open adversary!*
>
> *And he makes (meaningless) comparisons for us while forgetting his own creation (that he was created from nothing). He says, "Who can give life to dry bones especially once decomposed?" Say (reply to them by saying);*

He who created them the first time into existence shall give them life (again). For He is of all creation fully knowing!"

He is the One who produces fire out of the green tree then are you able to kindle fire for yourselves.

Is not the One who created the heaven and earth, fully able to create the likes of them (being that they are so much smaller and easier to create compared to the vastness of the heaven and the earth)? Yes, indeed he can for He is the Supreme Creator, the Supreme Intelligence!

Verily when He intends a thing, His command is, "Be", and it is!

Therefore, Glorified is the One in whose hands is dominion of all things and it is to Him you all shall return!"

(Quran 36:76-83)

This passage is sufficient for the real truth seeker to know without doubt that Allah will reincarnate us back in front of Him and judge our lives accordingly. The Arab who challenged the Prophet was silenced.

Such revelation from Allah not only fully refuted the false claims that there is no after life after this one, but also the false claims that one may hear from Hindus or Buddhists of us reincarnating into different forms of life (like as plant, animal, etc.) after this one – a cycle that combines eternally till we reach such a spiritual state to break free from the cycle altogether. Both chains are false. The truth has been clarified through Allah's direct words themselves in the Quran. We will die and then one day will collectively brought back before Allah. He will review our lives and as the ultimate Judge, will sentence us accordingly to Paradise or the Hell. Allah describes all these events with vivid detail, even telling us what people will be say on the day and also in Paradise and in Hell. Here's one passage capturing the deep regret people will have:

"(In falsehood will they be) until, when death comes to one amongst them and he says: "On my Lord! Send me back (to the world), so that I may work righteousness in all (the obligations) but I neglected!" (The reply will be "By no means (are you returning)! It is but mere words he (meaninglessly) says, and before them is a platform (not allowing them to return to their previous existence in the world or to move forward to another realm for now, they are stuck) till the Day they are all raised up.

Then when the (sacred) Trumpet is blown, there will be no more affiliation between each other on that day nor until anyone even ask of one another! Then those whose balance (of pure belief and righteous living) is heavy – They will attain ultimate success. But those whose balance will be light (they didn't believe or have enough care use their lives to invest in their afterlife accounts) will be those who have lost themselves (and their futures); in the Hell fire, forever they shall remain.

The fire will burn their faces off and thereafter (with deformed faces) shall grin, with their lips displaced. Were not my signs rehearsed to your but you yourselves denied them? They will say: "Our Lord! Our misfortune (of wickedness) overpowered us and we became an astray people. Our Lord! Bring us out of this: if we ever return (to our previous ways), then we will be self-oppressive people indeed. He will say: "Be driven into it (Hell with full humiliation) and do not speak to Me.

A part of My servants there was (amidst you all) who used to pray, "Our Lord! We believe so do forgive us and have mercy upon us, for You are the Most merciful of the merciful." But you treated them with ridicules so much so that you became totally needless of My Reminder while you were so busy laughing at them. I have rewarded them this day for their patience and constancy, these are indeed the ones that have attained ultimate Bliss.

He will say: "What number of years did you stay on Earth?" They will say "We stayed a day or part of a day, but ask those who keep account." You stayed not but a little if only you had known. Did you think that we had created you without purpose and that you all would never be brought back to us (for account)?

Therefore, exalted be Allah, The Ultimate King, The Ultimate Reality; There is one worthy of worship except He, The Lord of the Greater Throne of Honor! If anyone invokes on anyone other than Allah as a duty, such a person had no authority or proof thereof and certainly his accounting (for such miscalculation and wrong) will be with his Lord! Certainly the unbelievers will never succeed! So say: Oh my Lord! Forgive and have mercy verily You are the most merciful of the merciful."

(Quran 23: 99-118)

To Allah, who is beyond the limits of time and space, the future is just as certain as the past that was already happened. Thus Allah reveal to us one conversation He has on the Day of Judgement with Hell-bound people and paints the picture as if it is happening right here before our eyes. Try after try they keep begging Allah in their graves and on the Day of resurrection to get another chance. They promise Allah that if they are granted that change they will believe fully and act obediently, yet Allah sees through their claims and denies their motions of appeal, sending them to the fire that burns and disfigures their faces all instead, a punishment, they earned themselves for denying and making fun of the reminder and the believers who followed it. Perhaps the most spine chilling irony of the whole passage is that since its set in the future, there is possibility that anyone of us reading could be amongst those ill-fortuned people, Allah protect us! Thus the passage mentions righteous servants that always prayed to Allah for forgiveness and mercy, thus were rewarded and sent in paradise and the passage as well as the search ends by commanding us to also pray to Allah alone for forgiveness and mercy in hopes that we too be amongst those that attain ultimate success and bliss.

Why are we created? Why are we here on earth? It is the Day of Judgement that completed that answer full circle in the heart of a believer. We were created as spirits before Allah and then sent to the world in our earthly forms temporarily as a test to see if we would worship and serve Allah purely and obediently. Then we die and separated from our earthly bodies then we're resurrected before Allah, if we passed the test of life we are certainly rewarded in the Gardens of Paradise, yet if we fail we are sentenced to the fire of Hell.

So the purpose of life is Allah's service, and that Great Day is the unveiling and whether we fulfil our purpose and gained His favor or not, our simply put, eternal futures rest on however Allah-consciously live in this life.

The first transition we all will experience is of death itself, only later will we be resurrected together and judged individually before Allah.

"Every soul shall indeed taste death! And certainly on the Day of Long Standing shall you be paid your full wages (of what you earned in life). Therefore, whoever is saved from the fire (of Hell) and is given admission into the Gardens (of Paradise) had attained success (and the goal of life) indeed! And what is the life of this world except an enjoyment of delusion."

(Quran 3:185)

Death is the one experience that all humans know will happened to them yet it's one idea and truth that we least want to think about. The simple fact is that one day we shall separate from the very life we spend so many years to build up.

Death is the inescapable visitor that never fails to visit every single human being without knocking on our door. It is the heart-breaking visitor for most separating him/her from his loved ones, from the life he/she build up in the world, and from the very physical presence on this earth. Many a times it takes a death of a loved one for people to get deeper perspective on life and come back to Allah and his way of Islam sincerely and with a repentant heart.

What happens to a soul while in the grave? Angels come and test eh depth of faith of a person, revolving it around 3 central questions: Who is your Lord? Who is this man (displaying Muhammad S)? What is your way of life? If one lived Islam purely the answers from the depths of our consciousness will come easily. If not we won't be able to reply. Although the real accounting will be on the day we are raised, some form of reward and punishment will start as early as in the grave based once again on our beliefs and how we lived our lives.

The Day of Judgement has been called many names by Allah. It is the Day of Distress (25:26), the Day people feel cheated upon (64:9), Day of Assembly (42:7), the Day of Gathering (50:44) , the Day Well-Known (56:50), the Day that will inevitably come to pass (56:1), the Day of Accounting (14:41), the Day of the overwhelming event, the Day of Sorting out (77:13), the Day of the Ultimate Reality (69-1-3), the Day of Truth (78:39), the Day of Spirit (Gabriel / Jibrael As) and the angels will row up in ranks before Allah, (78:38), the Day of No excuses (66:7), the Day you will only be recompensed based on what you did (66:7), the Day ever gone will hear a mighty blast (50:42), the Day of Coming Out (and one's graves((50:92), a Mighty Day where all of mankind shall stand before the Lord of the Worlds (83:5-6), the Day that the clouds will split apart the sky and the angels shall be bent down descending (25:25), the Day the Trumpet will be blown (78:18), the big Day the mountains shall vanish as it they were a mirage (78:20), the Day of the Great Strike (101:1), the Day of the Great Earthquake (99:1), the Day that the people of Paradise are granted peace and joy in Paradise (36:58), the Day the Shatians and disbelievers are cast and thrown into Hell (76:64), the Day where the final and total command belongs to Allah (82:17).

Why is the day so intense? It's not because Allah is out to get us, rather it's because all those who took life and this reality and Allah lightly will realize the gravity of what they did. It was Allah who out of love gave people chance after chance and message after message for them to come back in repentance and in obedience to His way. But it was out of their insolence and rebelliousness that majority of people still continued to deny his revelation or continued disobeying Him. And yet Allah, out of His own good nature, was fore bearing with most of us in our lives with the condition that if didn't fly ourselves then verily we'd face Allah's anger on the Great Day and beyond. It will be our own collective lies and sins that lead to the terror and intensity of the day.

On that day, the hearts of all of humanity will realize how great Allah was and always has been all this time. Even the atheist who denied Allah's existence all his life along with the Prophets who most deeply praised and served Allah will all be in awe of His mightiness, His greatness, and in fear of their futures. The wise take Allah seriously now and give Him full love and attention, not like others who stand in regret on that Day when it is too late to do so.

What else do we know about the Great Day from revelation and the Prophet's ﷺ teachings? We know that even after being raised up, Allah will be fully present and the angels will row up as if in a stadium where they are the spectators and we are the ones on the field.

Then the gate of Hell will be dragged out and what a monstrous sight it will be! Everyone shall disassociate from one another in fear of what their future will held – Allah forbid it be in Hell's fire.

For a long period, perhaps for years on end, Allah will leave us tarrying in such fear. It will get to the point where people start going in crowns to righteous people like Ibrahim (AS), E'sa (Jesus AS), Musa (AS), and others asking them to ask Allah to start the Judgement. The uncertainty will be killing everyone. Even these great leaders of humanity who Allah loves will be so fearful that they won't accept the plea of the people and will only worry about themselves and their safety there. The exception being Muhammad, the final messenger and most beloved to Allah, who accepts the plea and who prays to Allah and praises Him and begs Him to start the divinely legal proceedings. Eventually Allah does and the great fate of mankind and the proceedings that will lead to each person's eternal fate now beings.

It should be noted here that although it's called a "day," it is not a 24 hour day like we perceive on this earth. The day is called a day for it's that one big date in our lives where everything matters, the length is many years long and amongst the most torturing experiences that most humans will ever experience.

People will be segmented behind the leaders of the people that they followed. Each prophet will be ahead of his own follower.

The light of faith in one's heart will be outwardly manifested, so some will have glowing bright shining white faces and some will have gloomy saddened dark and demonic faces. Some of the so-called believers who claimed faith in the world but were in reality hypocritical, being part of the Muslim community for social benefits or just for the heck of it, will be forcefully separated from the believers, gathered together with the disbelievers.

The Prophet ﷺ on that day will be given a special pool of water only he can access. Through it he will take out water with his own hands and give water to drink for his chosen followers. He who gets blessed with such drink from his blessed hands will never feel thirsty again and will be forgiven and entered into Paradise. Not all the believers shall get this gift.

This is why at the end of hearing the call to prayer, the athaan, we Muslims pray:

"O Allah, Lord of this perfect call and the prayer to be offered, grant Muhammad the privilege (of intercession) and also the eminence, and resurrect him to the praised position that You have promised)."

For the Prophet ﷺ said that whosoever says this prayer after the athan, "...my intercession for him will be permitted on the Day of Resurrection."

(al-Bukhari, 589)

The people of Jannah will be honoured in many different ways on this Day while the rest of the world stares in jealousy. Many will be shaded under Allah's throne from the intense heat.

"Verily the Companions of the The Garden shall that Day be joyous in all they do. They and their associates will be under (cool) shade, reclining on Throne (of honor). (Every) fruit (to especially enjoy) will be there for them and they shall have whatever they call for. "Peace & safety!" – a word (of salutation and glad tiding) from a Lord Ever-Loving!"

(Quran 36:55-58)

After the initial universal intensity of the day, passages like the above show how Allah makes the whole area a noble reception experience for the believers and the people going to the Gardens of Paradise, leaving the others in regret for wasting their lives, pain as they suffer humiliation and punishment, fearful that they will be thrown into such a monstrosity of unimaginable destruction and hopelessness of the Hell they see, and deeply wishing that they were honoured and rewarded and joyous in the ranks of those believers right now.

Each person shall be called one by one before the King of All Kings for Judgement. A book will be brought forth with every good and bad deed in record in the person's life.

This is the moment of truth! Everything hangs on the line of this one meeting. Allah will review and look at it day by day action by action of what you did. With Hell in plain sight and witnessing of people who have already been sentenced and dragged in there, there is no more heart-wrenching and emotionally nerve-wrecking experience than Allah, creator of the heaven and the earth and all that exists, auditing out lives fully and thoroughly. Each person will have a different experience when they meet Allah. Some will face Allah's merciful and gentler side, whereas others will face His Just and severe side. All shall be dealt with fairness and anyone sentenced to punishment will have brought such to themselves and deserved it.

> *"What would Allah gain (and why would He) by punishing you all if you are grateful and believe? Allah is forever the Most-Appreciate the All-Knowing."*

> (Quran 4:147)

We beg and continuously pray Allah decrees us to be among those who experience His love and mercy and forgiveness on that Day!

The meeting with Allah, rather than just being a simple accounting and an interview, is more of what organizational psychologists call a multiple hurdle test. In large corporations especially, beyond just looking at a candidate and looking at his resume and his past accomplishments and experience many will also put the potential job candidate in multiple scenarios and situations and see how he/she faces in those challenges as part of their consideration in hiring the candidate. So for example a person who is applying for a high management position could be put in a pre-designed role-playing game where he has 5 employees, and has product that was supposed to launch in 2 hours but has employees that have messed up the distribution channels. He has 2 hours to fix the problem. In doing such a test, those who are looking to hire for the management position can see first-hand how the person faces different relevant criteria they are looking for: leadership, communication, conflict-resolving, problem-solving, and how he deals under stress. In this way they get a more thorough picture of the candidate.

Allah too has designed this Day as a fully thorough review of every candidate by putting multiple hurdles that test the two criteria that matter most to Him: faith in Him and goo righteous living.

Three specific events come to mind when thinking of the different tests Allah has designed.

Firstly, the Divine Scale will be brought forth and good deeds shall be actualized as physical weight. Bad deeds take away from the wright of the scale, and disbelief venders all the weight to disappear. Sort of like how people will measure a person's net worth by adding one's assets and subtracting all the debts he has, in the same way Allah has created this scale for people to see their spiritual net worth live while they are being reviewed to see if they, deserve forgiveness and entrance into the Gardens or not.

> *"Then as for the one who have a heavy scale, then he will have a well-pleasing (eternal) life! And as far the one who has light scale, then he will be in the Great Pit! And what*

will make you comprehend what The (Great) Pit is? (It is) a Fierce-Blazing Fire!"

(Quran101: 6-11)

Then when all is said and done for the individual accounting and Allah reviews a person's life as mercifully or as intensely as He pleases, then his/her book of deeds will be handed to the person. Those destined for Paradise will receive their book with their right hand signifying acceptance and righteousness, and those destined for Hell will receive their life's book of deeds with their left hand signifying rejection and wretchedness

"Then when one blast is sounded on The Trumpet, And the earth is moved along with the mountains, then they are crushed to powder with one stroke. On that Day shall the (Great) Event come to pass. And the sky will be ripped apart for on this Day it will be flimsy.

And the angels will be on its sides and eight (great angels) shall bear The Throne of Your Lord above them.

This is the day all will be revealed and not a single hidden secret (of yourself and what evil you did in your past earthly life) shall be hidden.

"Then as for the one who will be given his book (of deeds) on his right hand, he will exclaim (in joy); Here it is! Read my book (of my Allah-centered living)!

Certainly I thought (and lived) with conviction that my accounting would meet me (on this Great Day)! Therefore, he will (now and forever) be in a life of bliss. In a lush Garden in high. The fruits whereof (will hang in branches) low and near (and in comfortable reach).

(it will be said in celebration to him) "Eat and drink with full satisfaction, (all this reward) because of (the good) that you sent before you in the days long-gone.

Then as for he that will be given his book (and record) in his left hand, then he will say, (in after regret and fear) "Woe to me! How I wish my Record had never been given to me. And that I never had seen how (bad) my account (stood)! Woe to me! I wish I had been left (dead without being reincarnated), of no profit has been my wealth, and all my (worldly) power (and influence) has been reduced to nothing!"

(Then Allah will say sternly ☺ "Seize him and bind him all of you (angels), then (throw him and) burn him in the Blazing Fire. Then make him march in a chain the length of which is seventy cubits!

Certainly all this (humiliation and pain and torture) because he would not believe in Allah, the Great.

And he wouldn't (care enough to even) encourage feeding of those in need.

So on this day no friend does he have (to speak in his defence). Nor does he have any food except puss (the filth coming out of the washing of the wounds), which none but those in great error eat."

(Quran 69: 13-37)

The last hurdle is one which the Prophet ﷺ spoke about but that the Revelation of Quran itself doesn't have much mention of. That is none other than the Great Bridge (Siraat in Arabic). It will be a very long yet thin bridge across which will be a plane with the gates of Jannah, underneath of which will be the Hell-

Fire. Speed and ease of passing through will be based on the intensity of a person's faith and righteousness. Some beautiful and righteous believers will cross the bridge like lightening and at the speed of light. Others will inch their ways across. And yet many others will not be able to make it and will fall into the burning pit, the monstrous creation that Hell is.

This is one meaning of the Path and Bridge we call on 17 times a day at the bare minimum when we recite the sacred prayer of Al-Fatiha, the opening chapter of Quran.

> *"Guide us on and along (and keep us on) the straight way (the literally also firmly-established bridge), the way of those you have smoothened (the path) for, not those who've earned anger, nor those lost and astray"*

(Quran 1: 5-7)

Looking at it from one angle, the bridge reflects out life in the world. If we lived on the pure path of Islam, we will be on the pure path to cross the bridge and enter the Great Garden. This is the path of those whom Allah has blessed, the path of those whom Allah has smoothened for. Those who live to earn Allah's eternal anger or those who lived astray from the guidance will be those who messed up in living life and thus they will mess up when crossing the bridge and will unfortunately fall.

May Allah protect us from the pain and humiliation on that Day and make us among those who, out of our efforts and especially out of His mercy, are granted acceptance in all of these tests and are granted Jannah.

So much more could be said about the day such that volumes upon volumes are written, but for our purposes this overview will suffice. It's now time to explore a little more in depth the lives of those in the gardens and those in the fire.

JANNAH & JAHANNAM

The wise one is he who prepares for and is willing to sacrifice for his long-term future. There is a famous experiment in psychology where kids are tested on their will-power. One kid at a time is brought in a classroom and given a simple offer: they can have one marshmallow on the table now of if they wait a couple minutes till the researcher comes back they can have two marshmallows. It's a funny scene to see thereafter, most kids can't resist the temptation. Some ate the marshmallow on the table as soon as the researcher left. Other tried to cover their eyes and had their mouth-watering before they picked it up and at it. Only a handful of kids had the willpower to wait it out and get 2 marshmallows. When the researchers came back, they gave the students who resisted another repeat offer: if they waited a couple minutes till the researchers came back they could double their marshmallows again from 2 to 4 marshmallows. Majority decided to eat them anyways yet a few decided and followed through and get the deal.

The researchers then waited years till these kids grew up as adults to see where they were at in the life and to see if there were any significant life differences between those who could resist and those who couldn't. surprisingly those kids who waited turned out to not only be happier, but also had better test results, better wages, and more stable relationships. That one quality of being patient and more accurately described as being easily able to delay gratification for more benefit led to so many improvements in their worldly life.

The offer Allah gives to us is similar to this offer. We are the kinds told to stay away some marshmallows (avoiding thing in an unrighteous way), if we instead choose to spend that time in His way in this small span of this life, then we get eternal life in the joyous abode of Jannah, with all the marshmallows we want in there! But if we don't pass the test and lusted get deluded by the marshmallows in trout of us, He becomes our abode. This is the ultimate delayed gratification test and the stakes are far great than we can imagine. Those who have strong muscles of patience and delayed gratification not only get the best in this life but also in the afterlife provided he/she trusts Allah's words of Quran and lives hereby.

> *"Then Allah will deliver them from the evil of that day and will shed over them a Light and Beauty and a (blissful) joy.*
>
> *And because they were patient and constant, He will reward them with a Garden as well as (garments of) silk.*
>
> *Reclining in tit (the Garden) on raised through, they will neither experience the sun (and its excessive heat) nor will they ever experience excessive cold. And shades of the garden will come low over them, and the bunching (of fruit) there will hung low in humility. And among themselves will be passed round vessels of silver and goblets of crystal. Clear and made of white, listing its they will take their measures (according to their measure).*
>
> *And they will be given to drink there of a cup (of wine exists heavenly) mixed with ginger (from) a fountain there called 'Salsabil.'*

And round about them will (serve) youths of perpetual (youthfulness): If you saw them (and the amount of them all ready to serve) you'd think they were scattered pearls.

And when you look you'll see deep joy and a magnificent garments of live silk and (beautiful) heavy brocade as well as being adored with bracelets of solver! (To top it all of) their Lord will give them to drink a wine pure and holy! Certainly this is the bountiful for you, and your life's Endeavour (to live fruitfully) is appreciated."

(Quran 76:11-22)

The weather is perfect, the servants serve us the most delightful of drinks, the Banquet of the heavenly food is spread for us. Get yourself ready, this is going to be the blissful party of a lifetime, the party that lasts an eternity with the host being the Most Loving and Generous!

Who gets such honor, such a vast kingdom, such royal treatment, and such delight. None other than those who remained faithful and patient. Those who trusted their Lord's words, worked hard to constantly please Him, and waited the life of this world out to see their fruits of their actions. Allah grant us such honor!

The people of Hell on the other hand will get the opposite treatment.

"Truly Hell is a place of ambush for the transgressors, (it will be their final) destination: They will dwell there in for ages upon ages! Nothing cool shall they taste therein nor any drink! Except a boiling fluid and a murky filthy drink, fitting recompense (for such criminality)! (They will face such punishment) for they never expected accounting (for their heedless life), but rather they denied

and lied against our verses and signs. And all things we have preserved in a record (as evidence against them). Then taste you all (the painful fruits of your deeds). For no increase shall We give you all except an increase in punishment!"

(Quran 78: 21-30)

What an evil end! What pain and suffering! Allah save us from such humiliation!

"When they are cast therein, they will hear the (terrible) drawing in of its breath as it blazes forth! Bursting with fury: Every time a group is cast therein, its keepers ask (in pity), "Did not a warner come to you all (to warn about such a painful possible end and such a dreadful destructive imprisonment)?"

They will reply: "Yes indeed, a warner did come to us but we rejected him and said, "Allah never sent down anything (like you, on warner, claim): You are nothing but in a big delusion!

And then they will further (regretfully) say; Had we but listened and used our brains (to take heed of the warner Prophet and accept and follow His way), we wouldn't have been among the companions of the blazing fire (like we are now)."

(Quran 67: 7-10)

They were honest and admitted that Allah did indeed send Prophets as warners and as guides to save them from the fire and grant them access to the gardens instead. They chose the wrong decision and rejected and disobeyed them and thus eventually became the people of the fire.

Those people of the fire, regretting their lives could be any one of us. Think about that for a minute. That could be you saying those words of: "Had we but listened and used our brains we wouldn't be of the companions of the fire."

We must make the right choice so that it is not us just saying that. We must do everything it takes and leave no stone nurtured to prevent such of bad end for ourselves and our loved ones. The choice is ours: to believe and follow the Messenger and be saved or to reject him and be destroyed.

Who is the warner and guide, the Prophet and Messenger we were given by Allah to guide us to the way to the Gardens of Paradise and for away from the Hell-Fire? None other than Muhammad son of Abdullah, the final and greatest messenger of Allah, Salalahualihiwasalam (May Allah send prayers of honor and divine favor on Him).

KEEPING IT REAL

Now it's Your Turn:

1. Do you have a masjid near you? How much more often can you go in a week? Start scheduling more visits in your calendar! Go out to a masjid or spiritual center and start getting attached to their weekly reminders! It's circles like these as well as people and writings like these that keep us grounded on our real life purpose till we internalize it on our own. That's when truly will live for the sake of Allah alone. Just like we all gather before the masjid and stand together for prayer before Allah, one day we will all, believer and nonbeliever alike, be raised before Allah. Those who took the standing before Allah and that meeting serious in this life and prepared for it and put their best foot forward will end up successful, those who denied the day and

avoided the responsibility that preparing for it entailed shall be doomed.

2. As amazing as attaining the love and pleasure of Allah and entry into Jannah sounds, and as scary as being disgraced by Allah's disapproval and anger and being sentenced into Hell sounds, we all have our own challenges of how we are striving to get to Jannah success and prevent Hell failure. What is ONE primary thing that by changing you feel you can alter the course of your eternal future? How do you plan to commit and ensure you follow through?

3. Isn't it time to totally turn to Allah? Isn't it time to dedicate your whole why and life existence to this noble path? IF YOU DECIDE THIS NOW AND PRAY CONSTANTLY FOR SUCCESS HERE, YOU WILL FIND A WAY TO MAKE IT HAPPEN!! ALLAH WILL MAKE DOORS OPEN UP FOR YOU!

Reflection Questions:

1. Sit down for a little and get a journal out. Between you and yourself, write down where you are at right here right now.

What are good righteous actions you are doing or have done you are proud of?

What are sins and unrighteous actions you've done or are doing that you are scared of being accounted for?

What are missed debts (like missed obligatory prayers, zakah, debts you owe others) that you still have to fulfil?

How can you increase my good righteous actions?

How can you limit my unrighteous ones?

2. *"What would Allah gain (and why would He) by punishing you all if you are grateful and believe? Allah is forever the Most-Appreciate the All-Knowing."* (Quran 4:147)

Sometimes the image portrayed of Allah is one of a punishing Lord alone, one that has set many rules and laws and regulations for us and will punish us if we don't obey. Such a wrong conception makes people forget about Allah's love, Allah's mercy, Allah's balance within his justice, and how Allah WANTS us to succeed and that is why He has revealed us the way to gain His pleasure.

What would Allah gain by punishing you? For him, his lordship remains as is whether you are amongst the kings of Jannah or amongst the prisoners of Hell-fire. So reflect on his generosity of guiding you via the Quran and the way of the Prophet ﷺ.

3. How intense is Hell-fire? Could you even tolerate being there burning for 5 seconds? How long is duration of those in Hell-fire? Can you imagine the misery and despair present there?!

Save yourself from the fire my fellow believer, become righteous and leave no stone to please Allah starting today!

And reflect on how joyous is Jannah! How delighted all the prophets and all the righteous (and inshaAllah you too!) will be there. How the joys are beyond words! How Allah belittles the joys of this worlds and reminds us that the real honor, the real kingdoms, the real pleasures are awaiting those who lived for Him here! Are you on the right track to being one of those people? Don't miss the opportunity of a lifetime of entry into such a Garden and such a Kingdom, give your life back to Your Generous and Abudantly-Loving Creator!

THE CHOSEN ONE'S LIFE:
THE HEART AND STORY OF THE QURAN

The primary story of the Quran is the story of Muhammad, the Messenger of Allah ﷺ.

And so if there is any one chapter someone should at least read in this whole book it is this one!

What book on the Quran would be complete without recounting of its lofty messenger ﷺ?

What historian can't but stare in wonder of his impact, what honest spiritualist can but be in awe of his great presence, what moralist can't but praise his moral standards and teachings, what Muslim can't help but cry in love and longing at the gates of Madina ready to die for the beloved, ready to do anything to please the Chosen Messenger of Allah!

What an honor it is to mention his name and be amongst those who praise him ﷺ and His Lord! Cartoon and Videos of hate don't decrease his glory even by a drop!

For his honor comes directly from Allah, the creators of the heavens and earth who we all shall return to, while their hate comes from their ignorance. If the haters but knew, they too would be ready to kiss the feet of Muhammad ﷺ and follow his blessed way lovingly and wholeheartedly.

Most Muslims love him but fail to really understand the depths of who he was!

Who was he *really?* Why was he so significant? How did he live and carry out his life?

That's what this chapter is all about.

Let us explore ten different angles of what the Quran mentions about him.

1) Main receiver and audience being spoken to.

Say: 'Whoever is an enemy of Gabriel, indeed, he has brought it (the Quran) down by the permission of Allah to your heart, confirming what was before it and a guidance and glad tidings to the believers.'

(Quran 2:97)

But those who believe and work deeds of righteousness, and believe in the (Revelation) sent down to Muhammad - for it is the Truth from their Lord, - He will remove from them their ills and improve their condition.

(Quran 47:2)

On one end, this may be obvious. Muhammad ﷺ is the transmitter of the guidance. His role as a messenger is to receive and properly deliver what is. But on another end the status and position defined for him by Allah is much deeper and much greater.

The Quran shows us that the first audience that Allah is speaking to and addressing IS the Messenger of Allah ﷺ himself. In fact, one of the greatest praises and honors that Allah confers to the Prophet ﷺ out of love for him is to address Himself as "Your Lord," meaning Allah loves to introduce Himself and highlight the fact that He is the Lord of the Muhammad ﷺ.

Why is this important?

Allah is going to make an example and role model out of the same man that is going to deliver the message. He decides to make him face much of life's diverse challenges to show how the power of faith and righteousness can really empower one to enjoy the best of this life and the most success and happiness in the afterlife. In this way, humanity is taught how to live individual life and communal life along and how to create a beautiful society, through the lens of one who succeeded in all those regards.

2) To be believed and to learn from

"Believe in Allah and His Messenger , and spend from what He has entrusted you with; those of you who believe and donate will have a mighty reward."

(Quran 57:8)

"In the same way, we have sent unto you an apostle from among yourselves to convey unto you Our messages, and to cause you to grow in purity, and to impart unto you revelation and wisdom, and to teach you that which you knew not"

(Quran 2:151)

3) To be loved and respected

Anas narrates that the Prophet ﷺ said, "Whoever possesses the following three qualities will have the sweetness (delight) of faith:

1. **The one to whom Allah and His Messenger ﷺ becomes dearer than anything else.**
2. Who loves a person and he loves him only for Allah's sake.

   3. Who hates to revert to Atheism (disbelief) as he hates to be thrown into the fire." (Hadeeth, Sahih al-Bukhari 21)

The people most loved by me from amongst my Ummah would be those who would come after me but everyone amongst them would have the keenest desire to catch a glimpse of me even at the cost of his family and wealth. [Hadeeth, Sahih Muslim 2832]

4) To be obeyed

"It is not fitting for a Believer, man or woman, when a matter has been decided by Allah and His Messenger to have any option about their decision: if any one disobeys Allah and His Messenger, he is indeed on a clearly wrong Path."

(Quran33:36)

"Hence, accept [willingly] whatever the Apostle gives you [thereof], and refrain from [demanding] anything that he withholds from you; and remain conscious of God: for, verily, God is severe in retribution."

(Quran 59:7)

"Say [O Prophet]: "If you love God, follow me, [and] God will love you and forgive you your sins; for God is much-forgiving, a dispenser of grace."

(Quran 3:31)

Because he is receiving the guidance and living the guidance and being directed by Allah himself, his commands are put in equal line to Allah's commands.

This is why Muslims not only memorized and spread the Quran to the four corners of the earth, but also after the Prophet's death, we took great effort in collecting his directives and sayings and personal habits and stories(called "hadeeth"), and then spending equally as much time in creating an elaborate verification science called "jarh wata'deel" (literally meaning criticism and praise) meaning to be able to evaluate as best as humanly to create a system of credibility of the people who were giving testaments of what they heard and saw of the Prophet (verification of the hadeeth that were narrated and determining which ones are more authentic and which ones less). Thus the hadeeth are the second most important source after the Quran that we as Muslims utilize for our legal canon to learn the religion of Allah and how to live and conduct our lives according to how Allah wants us to.

5) A cleanser of society's darkness

"But those who believe and work deeds of righteousness, and believe in the (Revelation) sent down to Muhammad - for it is the Truth from their Lord,- He will remove from them their ills and improve their condition."

(Quran 47:2)

As we will see in the next chapter, the Prophet ﷺ brought about a moral revolution in the lives of his followers which later spread across the globe. It is his teachings, sent and directed by Allah, that were heavenly and touched the depths of ones soul and in all aspects of life.

And Allah promises in the above verse mentioned that those who truly believe in the revelation and work righteously, Allah will transform them and upgrade their condition!

6) An example and role model to be followed

"Verily, in the Messenger of Allah you have a good example for everyone who looks forward [with hope and awe] to Allah and the Last Day, and remembers Allah unceasingly."

(Quran 33:21)

He's our messenger! He's not only the One who received and delivered the message! He's the One that LIVED it!

7) Of Sublime Character filled with love and mercy

Muhammad ﷺ was selected as the Messenger of Allah and the Messenger chosen to deliver Allah's final revelation of the Quran. He is referred to and made inseparable from the message and the faith itself. Sometimes, when the enemies of Islam couldn't find anything to attack in the beautiful message and revelation of Islam, so then they would try to attack his character or persona to try to put down the name of Islam. But those closest to him knew him and his outstanding character.

Allah says,

""Noooon, (A sacred Arabic letter and sound Allah begins with in this chapter). By the pen and what is recorded.

You are not, by the grace of your Lord, mad or possessed (as your enemies foolishly and spitefully say). Rather certainly for you is a reward (waiting) without end! And certainly you have a character sublime and great!"

(Quran 68: 1-4)

His character stole the hearts of the Arabs and non-Arabs alike. Once a Jewish man came in between his entourage and came up to him and shook him physically by his shirt collar distressing the Muslims around him and making them ready to retaliate at the Jewish man. The Prophet ﷺ forgave him and commanded he be given what he is demanding. Then the Jewish man revealed that he was actually a respectable scholar among the Jews and that he was just testing Muhammad ﷺ if he had the signs of the coming prophet prophesized who also had the quality of forbearing others. The Jewish man smiled that all the signs were confirmed in him ﷺ and then he converted to Islam.

"Verily, Allah and His angels send their prayers (attentive bestowals of grace and love and honor and blessing and support) upon the Prophet: [hence,] O you who have attained to faith, bless him and give yourselves up [to his guidance] in utter self-surrender!"

(Quran 33:56)

8) A witness & a savior

"And so We have made you a median nation, in order that you will be a witness above the people, and that the Messenger be a witness above you. We did not change the direction that you were facing except that We might know who followed the Messenger from him who turned on both his heels." (Quran 2:143)

Allah here highlights that the Prophet ﷺ is a witness for or against us and that we, by following his way, will be a witness for the rest of mankind that the message was delivered and was followed. Allah even mentions that one of the reason for switching the direction we face for prayer from Jerusalem to Makkah was to see who would be loyal to Muhammad ﷺ. He was the savior of humanity, prophecized to come to guide humanity out of their ignorance and darkness. And he did just that.

On the Day of Judgement even the nonbelievers will give testimony to that. We have recounted the intense seen of the day of judgement before, but will now mention Rasulullah's ﷺ exact words as recounts how all of humanity turns to Him to plead before Allah to start the day of judgement when even the other noble prophets refuse in fear and send the people to other prophets. This will show us that from the very inception of the Great Day, Allah will make clear the position Muhammad ﷺ has over everyone else in his courts. The people will then go and plead Jesus (AS) to intercede before Allah, and "Jesus will not mention any sin, but will say, 'Myself! Myself! Myself! Go to someone else; go to Muhammad.' So they will come to me and say, 'O Muhammad ! You are Allah's Messenger (ﷺ) and the last of the prophets, and Allah forgave your early and late sins. (Please) intercede for us with your Lord. Don't you see in what state we are?" The Prophet (ﷺ) added, "Then I will go beneath Allah's Throne and fall in prostration before my Lord. And then Allah will guide me to such praises and glorification to Him as He has never guided anybody else before me. Then it will be said, 'O Muhammad ﷺ Raise your head. Ask, and it will be granted. Intercede and It (your intercession) will be accepted.' So I will raise my head and Say, 'My followers, O my Lord! My followers, O my Lord'. It will be said, 'O Muhammadﷺ ! Let those of your followers who have no accounts, enter through such a gate of the gates of Paradise as lies on the right; and they will share the other gates with the people." The Prophet (ﷺ) further said, "By Him in Whose Hand my soul is, the distance between every two gate-posts of Paradise is like the distance between Mecca and Busra (in Sham). (Hadeeth, Sahih al-Bukhari 4712)

9) A man we can relate our life to

After all the deserved praise of his great spiritual and moral and historical stature, we come back down to remember that Allah, sent him as man out of His mercy for us so we can easily relate to the final prophet and chief of all creation ﷺ. He walked. He talked. He married. He smiled. He cried. He went through hardship. He saw such beautiful moments in his life and such lowly moments. And all in all, he showed what it means to be a true servant of Allah, totally trusting, totally surrendering to the Might that does and knows all. We will explore this dimension more in the next section when going over his ﷺ biography briefly.

We conclude this section with the beautiful words of Sheikh Yahya Ibrahim:

"From a distance you notice his eyes – piercing, brilliant and engaging. The choicest Praise and Mercy of Allah be upon him. Muhammed ﷺ, the Praised one is Ahmed, the greatest in Praise of Allah; sublimely appropriate. Al-Mustapha, the Divinely Chosen, is real. He was flesh and blood. Human. I love him, O Allah, I love him ﷺ. In a world of distortion, where truth is overcome by fiction, the full moon rises. Although obscured by shadows or an overcast sky, the moon remains. Such is the fame and honour of Muhammed, ﷺ. Of average height, he towers above the elite of history. He would stand fully erect without a lazy slump. He was powerful, ﷺ. His chest was broad with a dusting of hair that extended vertically in a thin line down to his flat stomach, ﷺ. Any kind of hardships you can envision and pray to never face was shouldered by him, ﷺ, simultaneously. He experienced in his 63 years of blessed life more tribulation than a cohort. He, ﷺ, was an orphan, a widower, battle scarred, and unjustly outcast. He outlived many of his children and buried some of his grandchildren. His uncle, the Mercy of Allah be upon him, was martyred and his body desecrated. He, ﷺ, was defamed, mocked, lied to and lied about. He was poisoned, stoned, and had to witness his companions tortured on account of their faith in his Message, ﷺ. *Sabran*, remain steadfast in patience, O Family of Yasser; your destination is Paradise. His teaching was simple. Allah, the All Mighty, is the only One deserving of worship and devotion. All that we encounter is by His Command. No harm can befall without His Permission. His hair, ﷺ, was black and wavy. He liked to keep it longer in length, usually not past his earlobes. It contained a few gray strands, about 23 in number. With dark irises he could, by Divine Permission, view a world that was unseen. He had long, dark eyelashes that from a distance could be mistaken for kohl. He, ﷺ, would not avert his attention from a petitioner until their voice fell silent. His eyes would sleep but his heart was awake. His eyes never betrayed or invited treachery, ﷺ. The weakest, poorest and socially downtrodden would access him, ﷺ, as readily as the chieftains. He sheltered the needy, fed the hungry, protected the vulnerable, guarded the secrets and instructed the uninformed. He, ﷺ, was calm when others were agitated, loving when others were filled with hate, and polite when shown contempt. He, ﷺ, is the highest standard of character and the spring of Divinely ordained etiquette. His skin, ﷺ, was soft and naturally fragrant. His blessed hands were softer than silk and gave off the scent of aromatic musk. He was reddish in colour. He was not dark, nor was he pale. His skin was blemished with the seal of prophethood between his shoulder blades. He was proportional in all respects, ﷺ. In his prayer, he found comfort and pleasure. His voice quivered in awe of the All Mighty. When leading others, he would, for the most part, recite from al-Qisar (the short chapters). If he heard a child crying, he would cut the recitation short to relieve the parent of any distress. His, ﷺ, grandchildren would ride atop his back during his prostration, and he would not move until they felt content. His voice was measured, and he paused at the end of every verse. He would recite the Quran in various accents to accommodate all the dialects of his companions. When alone at night, he would pray. He would remain vigilant for half the night, sometimes more, sometimes less. When he recited a passage addressing Allah's Divine Mercy, he would stop and ask for it. If one of torment, he would seek protection from it, ﷺ. His face, ﷺ, was manifest beauty. His eyes were well set apart and covered by full brows. They were not sunk into his face or overtly protruding. His mouth smelled sweet, and his teeth were always clean and white. His saliva was a medicine and blessing, ﷺ. By the Grace of Allah, it was a cure to the blind, increase in food to the poor, and an ointment to the disfigured. He had a full, dark beard that obscured his slender long neck from a distance. His smile was radiant, ﷺ. He was soft spoken except when he sermonised on Friday. His voice was melodious and captivating. He spoke only when necessary and refrained from idle chit-chat. His, ﷺ, tongue was true. He loved to listen and would ask questions of those whom he instructed. He was modest and sensitive to the needs and feelings of others. He smiled and laughed often, seldom loudly. When he, ﷺ, was displeased, it could be read from his face. He never raised his hand against another living creature except during Divinely ordained battle. He, ﷺ, was courageous and led from the forefront. He stood in the ranks of his soldiers and faced the hardship they endured. He ate what they ate, slept where they slept and dressed as they dressed. He, ﷺ, was a man unlike the world has ever seen. He, ﷺ, dressed similar to his compatriots. He never owned a throne or regal markings to distinguish himself, ﷺ, from others. He would walk without an escort and disliked sentries being placed to guard him. He preferred neutral shades of white, green and black to clothe himself with. When he ate, it was never to his fill, and he always ate while sharing his food with others. He loved milk, dates and honey. His favourite dish was tharrid roasted mutton on buttered bread and broth. He, ﷺ, cared for the earth and despised wastefulness and corruption. He was a tree hugger LITERALLY. He loved animals and instructed his companions to show kindness to them. When a camel wept, he would stroke it and speak to it in hushed tones. When the tree whimpered, he paused his sermon and embraced its trunk, whispering to it soothing words of comfort. Animals took comfort in him, ﷺ. Today, his modality of life and tradition remain intact, preserved not only in print, but in conscious spirit. He loved us so much, ﷺ. He would think of those who would believe in him many generations after his generation and weep in longing and hope. He loved us more than some care to consider. Every Messenger of God was allowed a request that would be answered by Allah. All the Messengers utilised their invocation in the worldly life except for Muhammad, ﷺ. He, ﷺ, preserved his invocation to be intercession on the Day of Judgement for those who accept his message! None can truly claim faith until Muhammed, ﷺ is more beloved to them than their parents, spouse and children. To know him is to love him. To love him is to obey him. If he, ﷺ, was to walk into your life now, what would he think? O you who believe, send your greetings to Muhammad, ﷺ."

THE STORY OF THE UMMAH:

ESTABLISHING THE COMMUNITY OF QURAN

Now that we have gone over his position via Allah's eyes, let us give a brief overview of the biographical account of his life.

IT ALL STARTED IN MAKKAH:

Makkah was the cultural capital of the Arabs. Following the footsteps of their founder of Ibraheem, they would annually visit it for Pilgrimage. But they're pilgrimage was a very filthy one.

Apart from the hundreds of idols that they worshipped beside Allah, gambling, sex, fighting, nude, were all hallmarks of the Pilgrimage at the time. And killing baby girls, oppressing the poor and the foreign(especially black) people, was all regular for the town people. Far from what Ibraheem originally intended, Makkah was nothing short of the Las Vegas of Arabia at the time during the Pilgrimage. And in down season, Makkah was nothing short from the "hood" and "Wild West" of our time. The gang leaders were the law. Sex, drinking, partying, killing was common. And it was survival of the fittest between people and between tribes.

To the divided tribal Arabs, Makkah was the capital and the one place they all could go in peace. When Makkans did something or followed a trend, whether it be clothes or religious rituals or anything else, the rest of the Arabs would follow it.

Plus, with it's annual pilgrimage, it was like a huge tourist attraction with much business and trade and much cultural exchange happening there. And there were many Arabian accents and people that would come to Makkah when they needed to stop by. It was like the New York City of America in that sense.

But to the bigger nations, not only Makkah but all of Arabia was a big joke! Everything was so primitive and backward there compared to the advanced civilization in Persia, in Rome, in India, and in China. The Persians would even mock the Arabs calling them those loser "lizard eaters."

That was all soon to change for a new hero was born. A hero that Allah sent to humanity Himself.

IT'S A BOY!

Muhammad ﷺ was born in 570 CE in Makkah, Saudi Arabia. His childhood was filled with much tragedy and loneliness: his father died while his mother was still pregnant with him so he never saw his father in his life, his mother died when he was 6, his grandfather died at the age of 10. That's trauma squared for a little child.

But he lived on without any signs of depression. The deaths just caused him to question our purpose of living and how we should live for. The famous WHY am I here? Was planted in his heart.

Following his grandfather's death, he then started living with his uncle at age 10. For the next 30 years, he lived an atypical Arabian lifestyle. First was him growing up a healthy young boy that knew about war and tribal feuds, who knew swimming and horse riding and archery, who was proud of his Arabic tongue and poetry, who was illiterate because Arabs were slow to the reading program. Then he grew and had to face the next challenges of life, money and marriage.

Some reports had that he offered his hand to his cousin that he grew up with, but she and her father rejected since he didn't have much financial security as they preferred.

He ﷺ started his own business and hired someone himself. Then he got a job offer that was more lucrative so he accepted it. The manager of the company he was working for was a famous and wealthy business women who everyone respected in the community. She was like a type of Oprah for the Makkan Arabs. Her husband had died along the way, so she was single and men would often propose to her but would get rejected. She was probably tired of "gold

But after months of working with Muhammad ﷺ, this manager of the company was so impressed by Muhammad ﷺ. His honesty and his work ethic was impeccable! She finally decided that Muhammad ﷺ, although much younger than him, was the right man to marry. But she was worried. Would he accept? What if he thinks I'm too old? What if he's not interested? Were all probably thoughts in her mind.

She sent her best friend to ask Muhammad ﷺ if he was interested in marriage. And after slowly leading him, she asked her friend to send the proposal (It was an Arab custom for respected women to not "preserve their honor" and not ask proposals directly)

To her surprise and her joy, he accepted!

At the age of 25, Muhammad was officially married to Khadijah. The whole of Makkah was excited and their wedding day was a happy day for everybody. People had been wondering who Khadijah would marry, and they were not surprised when they chose the Al-ameen of the town, Muhammad ﷺ.

What was to follow that wedding day was a love filled romantic and beautiful relationship. If men are made when they find their soulmates, Muhammad ﷺ became a man when he found his soulmate: his beloved Khadijah. If women become queens when they find their princes, Khadijah had founder her prince: Muhammad.

Life was good. From age 25 onwards, Muhammad ﷺ had many kids whom he loved dearly. He was financially free and would help supervise the business. And he was madly in love.

But in those 40 years, there was one thing different about him than the rest. He sought the truth. He questioned the society around him and the way people were behaving. And this made the difference.

He was born in Makkah, he lived in Makkah, he loved Makkah, yet he did not blindly conform and follow the crowd. He never took part in the killing, or the fornication, or the oppression, or in the nude. And when it came to things that he could control, he would be the first to support causes of truth and service.

For example, once there was a poor traveler man who was being oppressed by those in power. He and many of his friends got together and created a "Justice League" to address the wrong. And they succeeded, and the oppressed man was joyous.

Or when it came to service, Muhammad ﷺ was the first to give when people asked for help, he was the first to offer his home when travelers would come, he was the one always trying to help others in whatever way he could.

Or another beautiful example: Once there was a dispute while they were rebuilding the ka'bah, the sacred structure that Ibrahim lifted up. All the tribal leaders were ready to fight with one another, and it might have turned into a decade long feud. But they took the decision to Muhammad, and took the matters at hand and decided something that soothed all of their hearts and solved the problem.

They were more than satisfied, for all of them trusted Muhammad ﷺ. They knew Muhammad ﷺ since he was a little boy and they knew him inside and outside. They knew was a man of character, and wasn't there to fight for power or for rule. They knew he was just a genuine simpleton, who didn't know what lying was, and who was simply living the best moral life he could.

Amongst all the vices of the city, he was committed to character. Amongst the darkness and emptiness that the Arabs were living, he was a bright light. And the people noticed it.

People loved him, people loved his wife, people respected his children. They would call him Al-Ameen, which meant the truthful and trustworthy and the one we can always depend on. Truly Muhammad ﷺ and his love for the people and people's love for him was a truly beautiful scene. And he, nor they, ever thought the love would ever change.

A MOUNTAIN ON HIS SHOULDERS....

Every year, people from all over Arabia came to the Pilgrimage. And he was part of the noble family and tribe, who were respected by all the Arabs, that would take care of running the ka'bah and running the ceremonies and running the whole Pilgrimage.

"Why am I here? Is this what God really wants?"

The questions were bubbling and kept growing every year especially when he saw the people doing the Pilgrimage and worshipping idols all so blindly. The questions troubled him so greatly, he felt it was time he took some quiet time to reflect on this. Some reports say that from around age 27(2 years after his marriage), these questions and the confusion plagued him so much that he started going on retreats in the mountains. Khadijah would back him food and he would go hiking to a quiet untouched place in the mountains and sit there to reflect. Khadijah didn't mind, she was always by his side and knew he was an honorable man that was saying he was going to do what he said he would.

Muhammad ﷺ finally found a favorite place that he started making his retreat location, which was the Cave of Hira. It was a 3 hour hike up to the mountain to get there, which although was a bit tiresome, was perfect for the solitude that he wanted. He started staying there first for hours, then for parts of the day, then for days straight.

Sitting alone in the cave for days, the same questions came over and over.

"Why do I exist? Who am I? What is this world and universe around me? Who are you God? What do you want from me?"

This going out to the cave for meditative self-reflection and deep thought continued on for years and years and years. Along the reflection, he was also remembering Allah and doing dhikr, for from day one his pure nature made him always believe in Allah and because of that he never worshipped anything but Him.

But still this was a mid-life crisis embedded in the quest for the reality of the universe. And yet, instead of answers coming, the questions got more intense to the point of sadness. His mind just went deeper into circles revolving around the question of how do we really know.

"HOW do I know what is true? How do I KNOW what is right? HOW do I KNOW what to do?"

And then one day, amidst the darkness and loneliness, IT happened…

THE ANSWERS REVEALED,

THE SECRETS UNLOCKED

The heart was beating. The tears were rolling.

That one night, the pain felt more intense then it ever had before… and the ringing thought came once again to his mind as he was looking at reflecting at reality and thinking of the creator of reality, "What? Why? How?"…The dark empty cave all alone.

Suddenly, OUT OF NOWHERE, a bright blinding light came in the cave!

Muhammad ﷺ jumped in fear!

The *creature* quickly grabbed hold of him by his chest!

Without wasting a second, he squeezed Muhammad ﷺ by his chest and said in a loud thunderous voice IQRA! (RECITE!)

"Maa ana biqari'" ["WHAT DO I RECITE?!"] Muhammad ﷺ wailed in pain…..

AGAIN, he was squeezed so hard again with extra pain on his heart and chest! "RECITE!!!" the being commanded in his thunderous voice!

"WHAT DO I RECITE??!!!!" Muhammad ﷺ, full of tears, yelled again in pain. He didn't know what was going on, he just knew he could barely breathe and was about to lose his consciousness and was maybe about die.

He wanted to just listen to the perpetrator and have him let him go!

The being didn't bulge…and although Muhammad ﷺ was a great strong man and a wrestler, he couldn't move him an inch…the panting continued.

 "IQRA!! (RECITE!!!)" the being commanded as he squeezed again.

He was squeezed HARDER than both times before!

Before Muhammad ﷺ could reply, He softened his grip a little…Muhammad ﷺ let out a little sigh of relief and then the being said poetically:

"IQRA (Recite) in the name of Your Lord that Has Created! Who created man from a small drop.

Recite! for Your Lord is Most Generous! The One who taught man with the use of pen (and gave him the ability to record knowledge and access it again with it)! Who taught man all the things he knew not!"

Muhammad's ﷺ eyes bulged…what did this all mean?!!!

The thing let his grip go of Muhammad ﷺ …Muhammad ﷺ didn't wait even half a second… he ran as fast as he could outside and down the mountain. He didn't want to mess with whoever

Or whatever this thing was.

He was startled to death…a thing just appeared in the cave…was he going crazy?!! Was he mad??! Was he the target of something dangerous??!!

THE WISE MONK WHO KNEW

When Muhammad ﷺ went to his house he quickly rushed and told his beloved wife Khadijah to cover him up. He was shivering scared under his blanket. Khadijah was surprised! Muhammad ﷺ was always a peaceful man, and when he would come back from his retreats he would be more deep and casual. This was the first. When she touched him, she noticed the cold sweat he had-- Sweat that comes during times of fear. She knew something dangerous had happened to him. He was afraid that something was wrong with him or that something bad was about to happen to him or that someone was out to get him.

Muhammad ﷺ explained everything to her. Khadijah soothed his worries and said he could not be in danger, "By Allah, Allah will never disgrace you. You keep good relations with your family and relatives, you help the poor and the destitute, you serve your guests generously and you assist those who are going through rough times!"

It was for examples such as these that Muhammad ﷺ never forgot the kindness of Khadijah. And Khadijah was a smart woman, soon everyone would find out the truth behind the event.

Khadijah had a distant cousin that was much older than her in age that she trusted. She promised she would go with Muhammad ﷺ the next day so they could inquire about the incident and what it really meant.

When they set out and met Waraqah, Khadijah said, "Oh cousin! Listen to the story of your nephew (Muhammad ﷺ)!"

Waraqah replied, "Oh nephew! What have you seen?"

Muhammad ﷺ told him the whole story from end to finish. When he was done, Waraqah replied, "Surely, this angel is the same one that was sent down to Musa!"

An angel? Musa? Muhammad ﷺ was shocked. Waraqah then told him about the Christian prophecies about a chosen prophet that would come after Jesus. He said Muhammad ﷺ was the chosen one that he and the Christians were waiting for all of these years! That the words that the angel said were actually part of revelation directly from Allah!

And then he lamented his old age saying he wished he were younger so he could be around when Muhammad ﷺ would be expelled by his people.

Muhammad ﷺ was already in awe. He had no idea of what to say or if this cousin of Khadijah's was right. And the last statement was the most shocking of all. Expelled? But they loved and respected him in Makkah, it was his hometown and the hometown of his ancestors!

"Will they expel me?" Muhammad ﷺ asked Waraqah.

"Yes," the wise monk said, "No man is sent with what you have been sent without being treated with hostility."

For centuries, people awaited the final messenger. All the prophets were taught about him and Jesus specifically tells his followers to await his coming and mentions him by name. Even in the Old Testament he is clearly prophesized as the Prophet from the children of Kedar(Arabs) that will bring faith to the Gentiles. This is mentioned in the Christian and Jewish Bible and for those curious, do check it out in Isaiah 42.

Just like Jesus, Moses, and other prophets, he too came from the blessed lineage of Prophet Abraham.

His father passed before his birth, his mother at the tender age of 6, and his grandfather who held custody of him after his mother's passing died when he was 10 years of age.

Even at a young age the Prophet ﷺ had faced loss of his loved ones just like Yusuf (AS) did, deepening his trust with the One that was there for him all this time and even during those heart breaking times, Allah himself. At age 10, his uncle Abu Talib took him ﷺ under his house. At 25 he got married to a rich and dignified noble woman name Khadijah, with whom he bore many children and with whom he had a blissful and faithful marriage that lasted around 28 years until here passing (May Allah be pleased with her).

He lived a regular life up until his 40th year, having a wonderful marriage and having wonderful children, and gaining dignity and respect in the whole tribe of Makkah that he was a part of.

Muhammad ﷺ had a stable life of dignity but started questioning deep metaphysical questions and problems of his society more and more. He especially became fond of long periods of silence of meditation in the outskirt mountain of Makkah. One night, while alone in the cave of Hira, he meditated deeper and deeper. He already knew of the One Creator and he already experienced oneness with nature and the universe, but his heart was consumed in wanting to know what Allah wanted of him and what Allah planned of him & the world. Who was Allah really? What does he want from me and society? What will happen to us after I die? Questions like these must have babbled constantly through his head, weighing down heavy on his heat.

APPOINTED AS THE FINAL MESSENGER

Then it happened. The deep silence of the cave and the darkest therein broke! A being of light approached out of nowhere. Startled Muhammad ﷺ Jumped. Scared for his life, he considered running. But it was too late.

The being grabbed hold of him and squeezed his life away. As he squeezed him he said with a mighty powerful voice "Iqra", which meant "Recite!" "I am not among the reciters" pointed Muhammad ﷺ as he breathed what he felt like were his last breathe on earth. Again he squeezed with full vigor echoing the same command, "Recite!" With tears in his eyes he said again, "I'm not one of the reciters!" While struggling to try to get out of his unshakeable grip, the being says again, "Recite!" For a third and a last time he desperately said in ache and with a tone of desperation, "I'm not one of the reciters!"

Then the being said in a powerful divinely rhythmic melody the Arabic words which mean: "Recite in the name of your Lord, the one who created! He created mankind out a clinging clot. Recite! And your Lord is Most Bountiful, who taught by the pen, taught mankind which they did not previously know."

The words were profound such that Muhammad's ﷺ eyes widened, what did it mean? Recite what? Who is the one squeezing?

Then the being released him, and Muhammad ﷺ, in fear of his life, darted out, hiked speedily down the mountain and rushed home filled in sweat and shocked and confused at what happened, was he going mad? Eventually it was made known to him that the being was angel Jibraeel (Gabriel) (AS) who by virtue of that first revelation of Allah's words, conferred to him the mantle of prophethood.

RELYING ON ALLAH AND STAYING RESILIENT

For 13 years thereafter he remained in Makkah preaching Islam and spreading the words of Allah that were slowly revealed to him. Unfortunately though things got progressively worse for him and his followers since the persecution from the nonbelievers increased. They found his message of believing and worshipping one God alone, rejecting all idols or other gods as worship, honoring family and the poor and weak, being fair in your economic dealings, and that there is a Day of Judgement and an afterlife we all will gather at as too radical and as being too big of a threat to their power and authority. Thus the Quraysh, the strongest tribe in Arabia and the tribe the Prophet S himself belonged to, continued to harass the Muslims. What started as just jeering and taunting turned into organized killing, public beatings and public shamings to the weak Muslims.

HEARTBREAK OF MAKKAH

For almost 13 years after revelation descended, he kept calling the people towards Islam. These weren't just any people, these were HIS people!

The same people that loved him and praised him so much all of these years.

For two years after, Islam was kept undercover and only in private circles.

Finally, Allah commanded Muhammad ﷺ to go public.

The Prophet went to Mount Safa, situated in the rustling bustling center of town, and then gave the EMERGENCY call of the town. Sort of like the fire alarms of today and as is true even of many animal tribes, tribes had emergency calls at the time in case a warring tribe was coming or if danger was imminent.

When the call was heard, everyone stopped what they were doing and would go to the caller to hear what the danger was.

Muhammad ﷺ was nervous. He feared what people would say to him. He was always respected in the community, but was a bit more introverted. But this was Allah commanding him to go public, and he was always full force in obeying His Beloved.

Sometimes there were false emergency alarms, but when people saw it was Muhammad ﷺ doing the call they were all stressed about what's going on!

"Oh my people! If I tell you that beyond this mountain there is an army about to invade, will you believe me?"

All of them replied with great trust,

"OF COURSE WE'LL BELIEVE YOU, YOU'VE ALWAYS SPOKEN THE TRUTH!"

He then felt a relief and said to the people:

"Then I stand here before you, to tell you that the army of death is after you! I warn you of a great punishment of Allah imminent! I am Allah's Messenger! Accept me(as a Messenger) and believe (this message)! Give up worshipping idols, worship Allah alone! Obey His commands! And Leave evil actions so you may all attain salvation and safety(from Allah's punishment)!"

The crowd was shocked and speechless. Should they believe in him and become Muslim? They were waiting for the elite ruler tribesmen to make the first move and reply.

An awkward silence appeared with everyone looking at one another....till Abu Lahab, the Prophet's uncle, broke the silence.

Unfortunately, and to his eternal regret, he denied the Message mockingly said to him, "May you perish Oh Muhammad ﷺ!!! Is this all you called us for?!!!"

They all dispersed and broke off, and the Prophet ﷺ was very disheartened. This was the start of a very deep conflict that was soon to occur in Makkah.

Many close people did convert, I mean it was Muhammad ﷺ inviting them to this religion, not just any random guy from the street!

But most did not. Many of his own family members were running the politics and the law in the town. To them, Muhammad ﷺ was a threat and was in it for power.

Al-Mubarakpuri eloquently captures their reaction and their reason for holding back in his Prophetic biography book called the Sealed Nectar. He says,

"The Makkans, on their part, burst into outrage and disapproval. Muhammad's Pbuh words created a thunderbolt that turned the Makkan time-honoured ideological life upside down. They could ill afford to hear someone attaching to polytheists and idolaters, the description of straying people. They started to rally their resources to settle down the affair, quell the onward marching revolution and deal a pre-emptive strike to its votaries before it devours and crushes down their consecrated traditions and long standing heritage. The Makkans had the deep conviction that denying godship to anyone save Allâh and that belief in the Divine Message and the Hereafter are interpreted in terms of complete compliance and absolute commitment, and this in turn leaves no area at all for them to claim authority over themselves and over their wealth, let alone their subordinates. In short, their arrogated religiously-based supremacy and highhandedness would no longer be in effect; their pleasures would be subordinated to the pleasures of Allâh and His Messenger and lastly they would have to abstain from incurring injustices on those whom they falsely deemed to be weak, and perpetrating dreadful sins in their everyday life."

The conflict continued for years. People were murdered and oppressed. Many were exiled.

It got so severe, that a huge group of them migrated to nearby Abyssinia (modern day Ethiopia) because the Christian king there (who later became Muslim) was very just.

Confrontation after confrontation, Muhammad ﷺ and his followers suffered a lot. And the situation just got worse and worse.

In between were a few days of happiness, like the day when the strong influential U'mar became a Muslim. But overall, the situation kept tensing.

The polytheistic idol worshipping Makkans had enough. Like Hitler's tactic for the Jews, Makkans now plotted to boycott the Muslims from basic necessities and throw them in a concentration camp. They succeeded.

The Year of Sorrow as it was called for the tragedies and losses faced, was one of the most painful depressing moments of his life.

First, the Prophet's ﷺ beloved wife of 28 years, Khadijah (R) physically weakened by the difficult last 3 years of difficulty, passed away. His oh so loyal wife that he'd been happily married for more than 25 years died in that year from harsh conditions. He shed his tears, and cried his heart out especially when Khadijah passed away. You can tell a man was deeply in love when for the rest of his life he would keep mentioning that same woman over and over again and praising her and awaiting to reunite with her and honoring her friends. That was Muhammad ﷺ for you. And these events were just glimpses of the deep affection and care he had for his beloved wife. Here was the woman who stood through thick and thin by the side at the Prophet ﷺ, who loved and believe in him before he was appointed with his lofty position, who consoled and reassured the Prophet even in those hard moments when he doubted himself, who married him even though he was much younger and he wasn't financially stable of the time, the woman who stole his heart and bore him his children was now gone.

Second, his uncle who gave him political protection and raised him up, Abu Talib, also passed. At this point, the woman who gave him emotional closure all these years as well as the man who gave him physical protection were both gone. But heartbroken and lonely as he felt for such deep personal losses of people he loved so much, he continued to gain the strength he needed from the One who was there with him whether in victory or loss, the One who was guiding him this whole time, the Loving who knew and heard his pain, the Wise who was designing his life for worldly and eternal success, the Lord of all creation for whose sake the prophet and his followers were traversing on this path.

THE LOWEST POINT: TAAIF

Even with these heavy losses there was no time to sit still, his community's future as well as his own life was increasing by getting more and more in jeopardy. For this reason, the Prophet ﷺ secretly visited the nearby town of Taaif to see if they could grant his community protection and asylum.

The Prophet, along with Zaid bin Haritha, undertook the mountainous journey on foot. This was done so that no suspicion was roused that Muhammad ﷺ was leaving Makkah.

When he reached Taif, Muhammad ﷺ went directly to the leaders and explained to them the message of Islam. The leaders not only rejected it, but they also ridiculed the Messenger and displayed horrible manners. As was the manner of the Prophet, he did not respond to foolish behavior. He got up to leave, while telling them to at least keep his visit a secret. The leaders of Taif did the opposite. They also set their young boys to chase the visitors with stones.

The pelting stones left the Prophet's ﷺ heels soaked with blood, as he and Zaid entered a garden to escape the chasing mob. The Prophet ﷺ took rest under a tree. And it was at this time that he made the heartfelt du'a to his Lord:

"O Allah, to you do I complain of the weakening of my strength, of my few options, of the way people humiliate me, O Most Merciful of the merciful ones. You are the Lord of the weak ones, and You are my Lord. To whom will You entrust me? To a distant (stranger) who will show me an unwelcoming face, or to an enemy, whom You have given control over my situation? If You are not angry with me, then I do not mind, though safety from You is easier for me. I seek refuge with the Light of Your Face, which brings light to darkness, and upon which the affairs of the world and the Hereafter become right – from Your anger descending upon me, or Your displeasure befalling me. I will continue to seek Your Pleasure, until You become pleased (with me). And there is neither might nor power except with You."

He was clearly anguished and tensed by the tough situation he was going through. Among all the difficulties he traversed through in this mission, the day of Taif was the heaviest on him, as he once recalled later in his life. But despite what he faced, it was not really problems that concerned him. What mattered to him was the pleasure of his Lord. "If You are not angry with me, then I do not mind..."

No sooner than he finished his supplication that Allah responded and sent angel Jibreel along with the angel of mountains. The angel was at his command to crush the people between the mountains. His people had rejected and harmed the Messenger of God, not any trivial deed to do. But the Prophet of Mercy instead prayed and hoped the progeny of those people would embrace Islam.

Instead of warmly welcoming him or even given him a decent civil meeting as any respectable leader would do, the whole community mobilized against him driving him out and insulting him and having the children pelt him with stones as he was leaving. Blood flowing through the body and being humiliated like never before on a trip that he hoped would bring an opening, the Messenger of Allah ﷺ was broken like never before and prayed to the All-Watching and All-Hearing for support in this moment of desperation. The prayer was answered, the tides were about to turn, through the blessings of 2 journeys that Allah blessed the Prophet to undertake very soon thereafter.

As bad as it was and as it was worse as it was getting, he remarkably, didn't give up hope. Or rather, he just couldn't give up hope.

He knew he was on a mission. And so he never complained once to Allah. He FACED the challenges, and he knew this whole life was just a test. He knew that there was light at the end of the tunnel. He knew Allah had his back.

Muhammad ﷺ now had no choice but to return back to Makkah, which would be life-threatening. The Quraish (leaders of Makkah) had learned about his apparent failure and thought it was the defeat of the Messenger of Allah.

"How can you enter (Makkah) when they have forced you to leave? And you went out seeking help, but you were not helped?" Zaid worriedly asks.

The Prophet ﷺ replies, *"O Zaid, indeed Allah will provide relief and a way out from (the situation) you see (right now). And indeed Allah will support and help His Religion, and will grant victory to His Prophet."*

Having no idea what the future had in store for him (yet having full trust in the Almighty whose messenger he was), he retired to the Cave of Hira before entering Makkah.

THE HIGHEST POINT: ISRA WA'MI'RAAJ!

After all of the hardship and sadness and ill fate he faced the past year including the toughest day of Taaif, Allah decided to give Rasulullah a special treat, one that he had never given any one else before or after him. You know when I work really hard for a few months or even for a few weeks on some project or on school I think to myself, "Man do I need a break and a vacation!"

Muhammad ﷺ hadn't had such a break for 10 years even though he had the hardest job. But this one night, Allah made it all up for him.

One night as Rasulullah was sleeping, and he heard something outside. When he went out to see what it was, it was none other than his angel friend Jibreel, the same angel that came in the Cave who would come down very frequently to send revelation to him and to teach him Islam.

With Jibreel was a horse like creature made of light. They departed in what was not only a journey of a lifetime, but a GREAT event of human history! In that journey, Muhammad ﷺ crossed the barriers of time and space. He traveled and flew from Makkah all the way to Jerusalem, and there he had special a welcoming team!

Who were they?

They were none other than ALL the other Prophets themselves! Muhammad's ﷺ heart was delighted. He was then asked to lead them all in the prayer, a respect like no other.

The journey was only beginning.

Muhammad ﷺ then went on the same horse of light, and went up up and away…As buzz lightyear would say, "To infinity and beyond!"

He crossed one heaven after the other, meeting Prophets and angels along the way.

He saw heaven and hell and the inmates in both.

He saw the severe punishments of the inmates of Hell and the great blissful rewards of the guests of Paradise.

Remember how we talked about Hajj being such a powerful sign and divine miracle and accepted act by Allah? Well turns out we are the only creatures that have such blessings!

The Prophet ﷺ witnessed Baitul ma'moor, a "much frequented house", which was the ka'bah of the angels! It was truly a sight to see! Tens of thousands of angels all circling together doing tawaaf like we do…subhanAllah(Glory be to Allah)!

It was a little before a tree they saw in the distance where Jibreel said he could no longer pass any farther…This was the place only Muhammad ﷺ could go past.

There Muhammad ﷺ went more up and closer till he finally reached a place called sidratul muntaha(The Lote Tree which none can pass farther from).

There Muhammad ﷺ met with His Lord Allah directly in the manner that only He and Muhammad ﷺ know best.

Now there is a lot of discussion on what Muhammad ﷺ saw and how far he saw and if he saw with real eyes of this world or spiritual eyes. All those discussions are pretty useless. I mean even in the Quran, the words Allah uses to describe the event are very esoteric. Why? Because we can't even fully grasp that the concept of a human being breaking the time-space continuum let alone what looking beyond that reality would look like. It was Allah who created this continuum and he can mold it and shape things and do things as He wishes. This event was a proof of this truth.

If there was any highlight of the Isra…it was Muhammad ﷺ finally meeting His Lord. Neither riding a creature made of light, nor leading all the Prophets in prayer, nor touring and seeing Masjid Al-Aqsa, nor seeing Jahannam and Jannah and the dwellers there, nor anything else compared to that meeting. He met Allah! The same Lord that revealed so much to Him, that supported him, that assisted him, that showed him things in the dreams. Now it wasn't belief anymore. It was him witnessing it firsthand. Can you imagine that thought?

That He ACTUALLY SAW Jannah. He SAW Jahannam. He SAW angels. He saw and Allah showed him so he could then inform us of what he saw. We'll soon see it too, but only after our deaths. Our job is to learn and then use that information that Rasulullah presented to us so that when we do see all that he saw, we are among the successful!

When he came back and related his story, the Makkan idol worshippers were high in happiness.

They wanted Muhammad ﷺ to spread the event's news so they could call him more of a mad man!

Creepily enough, Muhammad ﷺ said in vivid detail the description of all the caravans that were coming in Makkah's direction in the next few months that he saw while traveling to Palestine. He was on the dot with every detail he spoke about.

If that wasn't proof enough, Allah revealed chapter 53 in defense of the Prophet. The idol worshippers happiness soon faded, and the believer's spirits were cooled and re-inspired by the event! The heart did not lie [about] what it saw.(53:11)

THE HEAVENLY ASCENT

The first journey was of the highest of spiritual kinds, the bless night where the Messenger of Allah ﷺ travelled and eventually met his Lord, known as Al-Isra Wal Mi'raj (the journey and the ascension), the Prophet ﷺ woke up one night to find angel Jibreel (AS) and a horse- like creature made of light named Al-Buraq (Lightening) waiting for him outside.

Sitting on that otherworldly creature, the very dimensions of time and space were no longer limits for the Prophet (S). Time froze and travel even very long distances within a matter of seconds became easy. Einstein's theory of relatively posts and commutates ad confirmation of such an idea: if matter was able to travel the speed of light, tune itself would freeze for such matter. The Prophet ﷺ did just that, transcending the usual dimensions of space and time that he as a human being was limited too, for Allah, the creator of all space and time and all the things and events within that space and time, had special plants and a special treat for His Messenger ﷺ that night.

First the Prophet ﷺ was taken from the sacred city of Makkah to the sacred city of Jerusalem. He physically saw the caravans that were heading towards Makkah and those headed towards Jerusalem as well as the city itself. But on a higher spiritual realm veiled from regular human perception, the Prophet ﷺ when entering the sacred masjid of Al-Aqsa in Jerusalem, saw all the Prophets from the beginning time, thousands and thousands of them including Ibrahim (AS), and E'essa (AS), and Musa (AS), all lined up and smiling and awaiting his arrival, dignifying him and asking him to lead the ritual prayer that they could follow behind.

With humility before their Lord he led them all. In this way Allah comforted the Prophet ﷺ by showing him all the great men whose legacy he was continuing, men who also suffered great losses while trying to preach to the way of Allah. It also showed him first hand the dignity and support he had been given by Allah, for all the Prophets supported his mission knowing he was the last messenger, all of them recognized that although he was their younger counterpart, he was the greatest of them all and the one closest and most beloved of all to Allah.

The Prophet ﷺ thereafter ascended beyond earth's atmosphere and beyond the solar system and then even crossing the scientifically known universe's boundaries (what in Quranic terminology is known as the 1st sky).in this way he kept ascending past the 7 skies till he reached the higher realm.

Where the dungeon of Hell Fire and the Gardens of Paradise lay awaiting the Great Day they will be filled. A tour was given of both. The horrors of Hell and its tortures there as well as the great delights of Jannah and the royal treatment of those there the Prophet ﷺ had no words to describe. He was forever deeply affected by the witnessing of both sights – what he just heard about through Allah's revelation in the years past he was now witnessing directly with his own eyes.

The final destination for the Prophet ﷺ was none other than divine communion with His Beloved Allah Himself. Musa (AS) was honored by speaking to Allah at Mount Sinai, Muhammad ﷺ was honored even further by being called to ascend to peak to and to be honored by the highest of Divine

Presence conferred to any creation ever. Muhammad ﷺ was given status above them all, even Jibraeel (AS), the chief of all angels, stopped at the Sacred Lote Tree in that realm and told Muhammad ﷺ that only he himself had been given clearance to go beyond that point. Allah puts special emphasis in the Quran to no delve into the details of the meeting, besides stating that it was of the highest of transmission from Lord to servant, and of the highest of witnessing of Allah's divine sight and miracles. To speak any further than that or even to debate details like whether the Prophet ﷺ saw Allah directly with his own physical eyes or not are futile and pointless things to speak of, for we have no knowledge of the details of the great event beyond that was the most profound of experiences such that all of it was beyond words. This gave the Messenger of Allah ﷺ the stamp of approval as the most beloved creation of Allah and s the spiritual guide for all humanity.

> *"Allah did inspire to His servant what He inspired! The heart (of Muhammad) did not lie about what it witnessed! .... For truly did He see the Greatest signs of His Lord!"*

(Quran 53: 10-18)

The Prophet ﷺ was also given the gift of the obligation of 5 daily ritual prayers for himself and his community that if they also did would lead them to ascend to great spiritual heights.

"Raised to receive the injunction of ritual prayer, the Prophet ﷺ and his experience reveal what prayer must in essence be: a reminder of and an elevation toward the Most High, five times a day, in order to detach from oneself, from the world, and from illusions. The Miraj (the elevation during the Night Journey) is thus more simply an archetype of the spiritual experience; it is pregnant with the deep significance of prayer;

which, through the Eternal world, enables us to liberate our consciousness from the contingencies of space and time, and fully comprehend the meaning of life and Life".

(In the footsteps of the Prophet, Tariq Ramadan, p. 73-74)

The Prophet returned back home as a changed man. What were days or months or years in his journey was still just the same night on earth – He awaited till the morning to inform his followers of the journey.

When it was recounted, many of the nonbelievers enemies of Islam rejoiced. They felt like they had yet another reason to prove Muhammad ﷺ was crazy. How could a man possibly go to Jerusalem and come back, what usually takes months on end of that time all within one night's time? And to claim he ascended to the heavens thereafter that all a horse made of light? It sounded foolish to them and like a fairy tale. Some of the believers even fell into some doubts.

But Abu Bakr's (who was the closest companion and friend to the Prophet) conviction that if the Prophet (SA) said it was true as well as revelation thereafter from Allah confirmed and solidified the hearts of the believers. Their leader and the man in front of them that ate and drank and celebrated and spoke and struggled with them had just witnessed Paradise and Hell and met with the Prophets and with the Creator of all existence and then come back.

THE TURNING POINT: HIJRAH!

After many death threats and the situation intensifying, Muhammad ﷺ had to leave Makkah. There was no other choice.

Taaif had failed. But news was that the town of Madinah was becoming fond of Islam. Delegations from Madinah officially came and invited the Prophet and his community to move there in safety. The prophet accepted.

After much meticulous planning , first the Prophet's followers left for Madinah. Then finally Abu Bakr and the Prophet left. The Makkans were shocked that Muhammad miraculously got out of the city, for they had paid many spies and assassins to monitor him and bring him dead or alive for a huge reward of money. But Allah protects in ways we can sometimes not imagine.

Every day all the town's inhabitants would go out in the day awaiting the Prophet. But for almost a week, they had no luck and they returned to their homes saddened.

Finally one day, an active Jew in the community who had a high roof, spotted two black dots in the desert sand… "They're here! They're hear!" he roared in excitement!

The whole city got out…it WAS them!

And as he walked in the city, all the little girls were trained and were ready to sing in chorus!

They sang the beautiful words in Arabic which mean:

Oh the white moon rose over us From the valley of al-Wadā'gma and we owe it to show gratefulness Where the call is to Allah.

Where the call is to Allah.

Oh you who were raised among us Coming with a word to be obeyedYou have brought to this city nobleness Welcome best caller to Allah's way!

Welcome best caller to Allah's way!

It was a moment of great celebration. The community building that followed afterwards, the unity and love he spread between warring tribes, the laws of Islam that were now descending, the wars they had to go through just to establish Islam, the vibrant and charming community that was now running, and the Islam and the message of the Quran that was now the city's lifeblood…was all of the blessing from the Prophet's coming.

We will explore the story of Madinah in more details in a future chapter so we can learn practical lessons of community building from the story.

To say that this "Mayor" named Muhammad ﷺ cleaned up the city would be an understatement. Rather, he transformed what was a warring divided city into a capital of soon to be world empire! And all of that in 10 years and less due to Allah's power and guidance!

After years of oppression, Allah commanded the believers to fight back. A decisive victory at Badr put Madina on the map in Arabia. A partial loss at Uhud humbled the believers. The conspiring Jews who wanted Muhammad ﷺ out along with the Pagan Makkans and other Arabs attempted a grand battle to finish off the Muslims with a 10,000 strong army. By the grace of Allah, the Muslims dug a trench and survived. Eventually a truce was signed between the Pagan Makkans and the believers at Madina. This is when Islam spread most rapidly throughout the peninsula. The Pagans didn't live up to their word and broke the treaty. It had been 8 years since he had run away. Now it was time to march back to the homeland city, Makkah.

MUHAMMAD ﷺ RETURNS!

8 years after the Prophet was exiled from Makkah, he returned back there with an army of 10,000 Muslims that all surrounded the area.

It wasn't revenge. In fact it was the opposite. The Prophet had signed a peace treaty with the Makkans that included the Makkans not messing with some weak nearby tribes. The Makkans didn't listen. If there was anything that got Muhammad angry it was when people were unjust to others.

The same leaders that oppressed Muhammad ﷺ just 8 years earlier, were now going outside the city to where he was camped asking for forgiveness for him. It was always about them getting benefits.

On December 11ᵗʰ, 629 BC (which was Ramadan 20ᵗʰ, 8 year of Hijri) the Makkan conflict was over.

The Makkans saw 10,000 lights surrounding the whole city that night. They thought they were all going to be killed. The leaders came again, this time surrendering if Muhammad ﷺ agreed not to kill them.

Strange was Muhammad's ﷺ heart. I know Gandhi said an eye for an eye would make the whole world blind. But when someone takes your eye, and your other eye, then stabs you and spits on you, takes your property, then throws you in a valley concentration camp, then kicks you out, then has wars with you…and does that to not only you but spreads suffering for your whole community for so many years…all because your saying Allah is One without any partners or idols or intermediaries between him and that we all need to live lives of truth, justice, purity, and integrity….THAT'S WHEN taking at least one eye back is not only just but also fair and justified and a fitting payback.

Yet Muhammad ﷺ set the example. He let them go without thought. And in a historic moment he said the same words that Yusuf said. "Laa tathreeba a'laykumulyawm" Which means something like "Have no fear on this day!"

That was Muhammad's ﷺ way of saying, don't worry you're safe!

Now Makkah was ruled by Muslims!

How Allah turned the tables!

How marvelously he orchestrated the Prophet and the Prophet's community towards success!

Slowly, but surely Makkah was all converting to Islam. The idols were destroyed. The Ka'bah and Makkah that Ibraheem envisioned when he first built it was now restored by his very own descendant Muhammad.

Tears roll down in the Ka'bah and people come out from the sanctuary pure, because Muhammad ﷺ spent his whole life purifying it from shirk!! Don't forget all the lives, the pain, the tears, the torture, the oppression, the anguish, the wars, the evil that Rasulullah and his followers had to face JUST to practice Islam! JUST so you and I would have the deen in our hands! That is what our forefathers did for us!

Once Makkah became Muslim, it was nearing the Prophet's end. Makkah was the cultural center of the Arabs, so when the celebrity elite of Makkah started converting, the whole of Arabia started becoming Muslim.

Allah revealed these ayahs both congratulation Muhammad ﷺ and also foreshadowing that now the mission was complete on the earth and it was soon time to return:

> *"When the victory of Allah and the opening comes, and you see people embracing the Religion of Allah in (great) crowds, then exalt with the praise of your Lord and ask forgiveness from Him. Indeed, He is the One who turns (towards those who turn and repent to him)."*

(110:3)

DEATH

Imagine that you had a poor parent from humble origins… that gave their everything, even when it hurt them, just for your success. That was Muhammad ﷺ for all of us. Crying, going through oppression, going through wars, praying without end…for what? JUST FOR YOU and so ISLAM COULD REACH YOU! Now it's our turn to make him proud, to represent him, to live up to the Message he gave his life to deliver to us!

I can't do justice to explain his death. What a tragedy…the greatest that ever hit us as an ummah!

He was sick for many days, but everyone expected him to recover. Everyone was blinded by their love, so the possibility of him leaving the world never occurred to them.

Abu Bakr, Rasulullah's best friend, kissed his forehead and then went out and calmed the community down.

He recited the famous verse which struck the heart of the believers,

"Muhammad is only a messenger: many Were the messenger that passed away before him. If he died or were slain, will ye then Turn back on your heels? If any did turn back on his heels, not the least harm will he do to Allah; but Allah (on the other hand) will swiftly reward those who (serve Him) with gratitude."

(Quran 3:144)

For the people of Madinah, The most happiest day of their entire lives was when Rasulullah entered Madinah,

And the saddest day that they wept and mourned for the rest of their lives was the day of his departure!

And we cry since we love him so much yet were not able to see him!

And We cry at missing him and his loving presence :'(

And Yet we hope and long to reunite with him in Qiyamah as he awaits us by the pond! :')

And yet we hope Allah grants us eternal company with Him in highest levels of Heaven!

Muhammad: Allah's greatest gift to humanity in the history of this planet! Whilst all Prophets (upon whom be peace) were sent to a specific community of people, Allah sent him as a Messenger for all mankind. He brought to us the Divine miracle that still exists to this day, unchanged and sent directly from God: the Holy Qur'an. When he was wronged, he supplicated to Allah to forgive those who had tormented and tortured him. He bore it all with patience. He loved us - you, me, this entire generation - even though he had never met us. He loved us so much that whilst all the Prophets (upon whom be peace) were granted their various wishes, he saved his wish for Judgement Day, so that he could ask to intercede for his Ummah- us! His character and his appearance embodied perfect human attributes. He was gentle and kind and he loved all of creation, from humans to animals to the plants. Simply meeting him was enough for many to accept Islam; such was the beauty of Rasul Allah (salalaahu 'alaihi wa sallam). Those who love him, their faces and hearts are lit with light and they become reflections of his beauty! I pray that Allah increases our love for His beloved. Oh Allah, bless our Prophet Muhammad in every moment and in every day, endless blessings that do not cease until the end of time ♥♥♥♥

ISLAM THROUGHOUT THE GLOBE

After the Prophet ﷺ left us, the Islamic expansion continued and we became a global superpower. Everywhere the Muslims went, they brought the gift of the Quranic revelation with them, along their love of learning, beauty, arts, sciences, and of helping others. It was a global and moral renaissance for people the likes that human history has never seen before. Along the way, there were many hiccups and wars and battles as is natural of any empire. But it is a testimony to the divine blessing and mercy that was Muhammad ﷺ that to these day the verbatim words of Allah's as well as his are recited all over, and that the ummah of Muhammad ﷺ is so large, spanning from Africa to China and beyond.

A'LLAMAH IQBAL ON MUHAMMAD ﷺ

In the Muslim's heart is the name of Muhammad ﷺ,

All our glory is from the name of Muhammad ﷺ,

He slept on a mat of rushes,

But the crown of Chosroes was under his followers' feet.

He chose the nightly solitude of Mount Hira,

And he founded a nation, laws and government.

He passed many a night with sleepless eyes,

In order that the Millet may sleep on Chosroe's throne.

In the hour of battle, iron was melted by the flash of his sword,

In the hour of prayer, tears fell like rain from his eyes……

With the key of religion he opened the door of this world,

The womb of this world never bore his like….

We belong to Arabia and China and Persia,

Yet are the dew of one smiling dawn!

….The song of love for him fills my silent reed,

A hundred notes throb in my chest.

What to speak of the praise I sing of him,

Even the block of dry wood wept at parting from Him!

MUHAMMAD'S ﷺ LIFE STORY: CONCLUSION

You've now heard many people singing in praise and in love of him.

Why was he so great? What was his secret?

Many things could be said, but it all boils down to one thing that we mentioned in the earlier chapter: Muhammad ﷺ trusted in Allah! He recited, he listened he obeyed!

And for that he was honored by Allah, and for that he was raised in status.

The words of Allah were revealed down in his heart.

This was the final direct divine revelation being sent to humanity before the end of time.

This was the Message he lived for and died for, the Message he was sent to express in his life and deliver to humanity, called the Quran.

To conclude this section, I end with the powerful words of the famous French playwright, Alphonse de Lamartine:

> *"Philosopher, orator, apostle, legislator, warrior, conqueror of ideas, restorer of rational dogmas, of a cult without images, the founder of twenty terrestrial empires and of one spiritual empire: that is MUHAMMAD. As regards all the standards by which human greatness may be measured, we may well ask IS THERE ANY MAN GREATER THAN HE?"*

We reply loudly and proudly to his question:

SalAllahua'laihiwasalam! (May Allah shower his honor and light and prayers of peace and blessings on him!)

The Messenger of Allah, Muhammad, was THE best!

He is the spiritual father of the REST!

The Quran was revealed in HIS Chest!

With it he ACED life's test!

And that's why he was the most BLEST!

SalAllahua'laihiwasalam!

SalAllahua'laihiwasalam!

SalAllahua'laihiwasalam!

REALITY BEHIND THE SCENES:
THE 6 ARTICLES OF FAITH

The previous chapter was a chronological recounting of how the Muslims eventually established themselves as a community in the global stage under the leadership of the Prophet Muhammad (S). Even though historically that would have been miracle enough for a man in the middle of the desert to accomplish in 23 years, what was even more remarkable was that behind the scenes of the political dynamics, the Prophet (S) was establishing a spiritual order and a spiritual community of the deepest kind. Before the advent of the prophet and his mission, the Arabs in Makkah and Madinah and throughout the region were idol-worshippers, tribalistic, racist, killing and fighting for the most trivial of reasons, adultery and abuse of women was widespread, alcohol and intoxicants all over were the norm, and the most powerful men determined what the law was and thus they freely abused other according to their whim especially oppressing the weak and the poor.

Compare this to the scene that the city of Madinah at its heart and all of Arabia had become through the Prophet's work: rejecting all idols and worshipping and calling on One Allah alone, washing up and praying 5 times a day, fasting in the month of Ramadan annually, giving in charity constantly and at the bare minimum 2.5% of profit giving annually, going to Makkah for pilgrimage at least once in your life, the tribalism and racism was replaced with brotherhood and unity and fraternity under the banner of the faith, the alcohol and drugs and indecency was not only banned but the hearts were melted in revelation such that they preferred the high of prayer and meditation and the joys of decency and pure living instead, and now the law was based on what Allah and His messenger (S) established and a strong wealthy powerful man was just as accountable for his actions as a weak and poor man. Society had flipped 180 degrees from evil to good, from lawlessness to civility, from a life of emptiness and lonely desires to a life surrendered to Allah with the Quran's message and the Prophet's (S) way pat on tap. This was nothing short of a miracle from Allah for the world to witness and an immense blessing from Him to constantly guide and spiritually empower the community of His final revelation to reach such heights.

Let's now go through the fundamental beliefs, practices, and spirituality that the Prophet (S) preached, believe, witnessed, lived, and experienced, the very teaching his community learnt and made their own. It was this inner revolution that formed the basis for the outer revolution of righteous behaviour. And it's that revolution of personal integrity and commitment to Allah which led to the outer revolution of a redefined political and social system that took its historical stage then.

It's also important to realize that more than just a political leader the companions took the Prophet ﷺ as their spiritual guide to lead them to live a life pleasing Allah and reaching close proximity to Him and eventually to hopefully attaining eternal success by getting into Jannah through following his way. Every major religion has some level of a spiritual tradition that has continued on for centuries including, but here I'd like to compare the Prophet (S) and the Companions to the master and disciple relationship role that the Buddhists revolve their life around. A Buddhist will first determine which guru and spiritual master they'd like to follow or what their family already follows. Compare you can get a good idea of this level

of devotion if you think of modern day devoted Buddhist of Asia.

They'll share their heads, and down on simple (usually orange or red) robes, they'll join a temple and be initiated, they'll be taught a specific doctrine of belief and scripture and chants, and they must commit to an austere life completely revolving around meditation, putting away from the sensory pleasure including fine dressing and fine eating and fine arts altogether, for they have a goal to follow both in belief and practice the way of their master, with the foal to free themselves from suffering and to internally awaken with awareness of the source. If they breached the code of life set, they may be kicked out. The more devoted Sahabah (Companions) of the Prophet ﷺ wholeheartedly took the Prophet ﷺ in this way: he was the master of the all masters and so they revolved their lives around his teachings and his way (also called Sunnah in Arabic). Unlike the Buddhists, they chose the right way.

In its essence, the spiritual path of the Prophet ﷺ is the path of Islam, the way of surrender. Islam in its whole meaning is the way of life of surrendering your will and life to Allah in order to attain both wholeness and peace in living and to attain wholeness and peace eternally in the afterlife. Surrender to Allah's will be fully accepting everything as it is, surrender to Allah's revelation by believing in it therein, surrender to Allah's commands by fully obeying Him, surrender your heart and your life totally to Him.

BELIEFS

There are six fundamental metaphysical realities that the Prophet (S) taught as the essence of the creed and theology of Islam. They are:

1. Belief in Allah

2. Belief in Angels

3. Belief in the Books

4. Belief in the Prophets

5. Belief in the Last Day

6. Belief in Divine Decree

Let's go through each one as to clarify what we as Muslims, as followers of our master and guide Muhammad (S), believe in.

1) BELIEF IN ALLAH

The Prophet Muhammad (S) and we the community of believers follow him believe in Allah's existence with doubt, believing that He is the Eternal Creator of all, the Light of all

Existence, the All-Aware, the All-Knowing, the All-Doing, the Ultimate Judge of this life and the next, and the only divine being and only One worthy and deserving to be worshipped, One without any partners or associates or any child sharing in

His divine and total authority.

We believe and know that

Allah is the Eternal Creator, thus Allah had no beginning to His existence nor will He (glory be to Him) ever cease to exist, He created all other things, both physical and metaphysical, both this realm that we can perceive as well as all the other higher realms that we cannot fully perceive, and He created them with His full knowledge, power, and wisdom. Be in awe of the greatness of our Creator and the marvelousness of His creation, glorified is He, there is none like Him!

The Prophet (S) was always marvelling Allah's creative abilities that He saw reflected in the beauty of nature. The sky and oceans with their expansiveness, the green foliage growing different herbs, the little insects, the abundant fish, the diverse animals, the free birds, the deserts, the mountains, and everything in between all sang of Allah's glory to him S. Allah was the most beautiful he knew deep in his heart and was the best of artists too.

> *"The originator of the heavens and the earth: when He decrees and matter He simply says, "Be" and it is manifested".*

> (Q.2:117)

Allah is also the light of the heavens and the earth. Just like when film animations first came out, cartoon artists has to both plan up each scene and then projector projected a light through the scenes to make it come to life, in the same way and in a far greater sense Allah is both the creator of every reality and experience and the light that makes it all come to life. In some sense we are just thoughts of Allah manifested by Allah's light

Himself and returning back to the loving one and source of light at the end of our journey through existence ultimately emanating from this light.

Allah is the All-Aware of all realities, so even the smallest ant that walks in the black of the night and even the greatest of starts or any other small or big reality, physical or metaphysical, He is fully aware of. Allah is the All-Seeing, the All-Hearing, nothing escapes his perceptions for He is the All-Aware of all things and happenings.

He is the All-Knowing as well, and just as there is nothing we can know that the doesn't already know, there is also no thing that we don't know and are ignorant of that He doesn't already know. For example, we as humans are ignorant of all the happenings that will happen in the future but to Allah these are things He already fully knows to the point as if it has all already happened.

Allah is the All-Doing, and so even though we may feel like we are acting in our lives, the

ultimate puppeteer who is pulling all the strings of our life and of the universe is Allah. There is nothing beyond His power and control, and all are under His rule and command.

Allah is the final judge and will judge each of our lives according to His will and in accordance with the guidance of His own words of Quran He has sent. It is only Allah who has the final say of what our lives amount to, it is ultimately the who will either sentence us to the fire or give us admittance to His choice Gardens of Paradise.

Finally Allah is One and the only one to worship. His creating, His knowing, His heaving, His watching, His doing, His light,

His judging is far beyond any of our comprehension and is far above and greater than any of our abilities, thus He alone is the One we worship and He alone is the One we call on for help.

"Say He is Allah, the One.

Allah: the Eternal.

He has no children nor parents. And none is comparable into Him. Belief in Angels

(Q.112: 1-4)

2) BELIEF IN ANGELS

The Prophet (S) not only taught the belief in beings of light knowns as angles, he also interacted with them on a daily basis. The hidden world of the angels operating around us was opened up for him: He would speak with them, see them coming and going, and had a deep friendship with the chief of all angels and the one who would bring down revelation from Allah, Jibraeel AS.

Let us then go over the 3 key creatures of Allah that will make up the scene in the afterlife for us, humans, angels and jinns, and the key differences between them.

Humans are made of dirt and clay, jinn of smokeless fire, and angels are beings made of light. Humans and jinns have the free will to choose whether to obey Allah or not, whereas all angels obey Allah without question and praise and worship Him constantly. Humans and jinns are thus part in the challenge of life, and if we pass by believing and living righteously it is we who Allah will bless with the gardens of Paradise.

The angels are the keepers of the gardens and the guards of the fire and those that run the natural world behind the scenes based on Allah's commands, but they as such have no dilemma like we do of being at risk of burning in the Fire.

The revelation on the details of our forefather Adam AS and his life shed more light and clarity.

> *"It is We who (originally) created you all (from your forefather Adam AS) and gave your shape: then we bade the angels to prostate to Adam, they all prostated, except for Iblis, he refused to be of those who fell down in prostration."*

(Q.7:11)

Allah was already there during our creation of course, but what we learn is that Allah was with the supreme, society of His surrounding Himself with angels. As we learn from details in the 2nd Surah (Chapter) of the Quran, Allah almighty first spoke and let His intentions of creating man be known to the angels that were around him.

Adam and Hawa (Eve) were given honor and a special capacity of spiritual knowledge that even the intelligent and pure angels did not have the capacity to grow or obtain. Allah thus honoured Adam and told all to prostrate to Adam in honor and respect. Angels, as we have already learned don't ever disobey Allah. They all fall down without hesitation. But one being a jinn actually, who was given honor to be among the company of angels since he was so knowledgeably and righteous, refused to prostrate. He was arrogant, he was jealous, he was spiteful that this new guy in town named Adam AS was being given so much honor. In the lower worlds and with lonely humans and jinns a disobedience may be forgiven by Allah. But here, Iblis (who was later to be known as Shaytan) was in the highest of presence and was expected so highly of that he was in the inner circle of Allah and yet he disobeyed Allah. To Allah, it was simple: Don't look at what I'm commanding, look at who it sis, the Great and All-Powerful One, that is commanding you and obey. When Shaytan refused re realize his mistake and turn in repentance and instead showed arrogance and embitterment towards Adam and his future progeny, Allah cursed him with eternal damnation to the Fire, him and any else who in the future among human and jinn who ever follow him. Shaytan dedicated his life to misguiding us on the path as an act of revenge.

"He (Shaytan) said: "Because You have thrown me out, certainly I will lie wait for them on Your straight way. Then will I assault them from their front and their back and from their right and left. You will not find most of them grateful!

(Allah) said: "Get out of here despised and (forever) expelled! Certainly whoever amongst them follows you, I'll fill Hell with you all (stuffed) altogether!

"(Allah) said then to Adam) "Oh Adam! Dwell you and your wife in the garden and enjoy (everything therein) as you please but approach not this tree, lest you become one of those dark and unjust.

Then Shaytan began to whisper (and try to incite them) with his suggestions in order to expose them in shame like it hadn't been exposed before. He said: "Your Lord only forbade you this tree so you don't become angels or so you don't live eternally. And he swore to them both, that he was their sincere advisor. So by deceit he brought about their fall, when they both tasted of the tree, their privates were exposed and they began to sew leaves of the Garden to cover (their shame). And then their

Lord called onto them: "Did I not forbid you that tree, and tell you that Shaytan was an avowed enemy to you both?" They said: "Oh our Lord we have darkened and oppressed our own selves, if you don't forgive us and show us your mercy, we will be amongst those who lose (everything including eternal safety and Jannah). (Allah replied and) said: "Get down all of you each as each other's enemies (Shaytan vs Adam). On earth will be your dwelling place and your meant of livelihood for a while. He said: "Therein shall you live and therein shall you die and from it shall you be taken out (at last for final accounting).

(Q. 7:16-25)

This was how it all started for us Allah had already created the Earth, Paradise, angels, and others. Everything was ready and setup for the inception of man. And once he came into being physically, a long-lasting war had started between the evil jinn and humans, a war led by Shaytan himself against the people of Allah throughout the ages.

In terms of classification, it is important to note that we deem shaytan a jinn that was honoured and the fell so low and was not a fallen angel like those amongst Jews and Christians many believe.

Also not all jinn are evil and followers of Shaytan. Many are Muslims and follow what Allah has commanded of them and will enter Jannah (Paradise). Surah 72 in the Quran captures an incident where a group of jinn came across the Prophet (S) reciting Quran and amazed by the profoundness of the message and the heavenly spiritual energy they witnessed therein, repented for their past lives and surrendered their lives to the one, accepting Islam. Jinns live long lives, they marry, and they die too. They are impulsive creatures and can possess humans and other beings, shapeshift, and travel at amazing speeds. People who deal with real black magic and voodoo and pertain paganistic sacrificial rituals to gain certain powers or to hurt someone are in communication with jinns.

Angels are pure, more vast in number, and totally devoted in serving and remembering Allah. The chief of all angels is Jibreel (Gabriel As), who was the means Allah used to reveal the Quran down in its heavenly descent to the heart of the Prophet (S).

3) BELIEF IN THE SCRIPTURES

So how do we as humans know what Allah wants from us? That's where scripture comes in. To designated messengers like the Prophet Muhammad (S) and others. Allah reveals down sacred words of scripture. They contain message of His oneness and who He is, divine commands, and sacred history of the past. The Quran is chief revelation amongst them all & the final one. There are countless others revealed throughout human history, but key ones mentioned are the Zaboor (Psalms) revealed to Dawood (David AS), the Tawrah revealed to Musa AS and the Injeel revealed to E'sa (Jesus AS). The Old Testament and New Testament and other scriptures of today we believe to be tempered with by humans, thus another reason why there was historic need for a Quran to be revealed in order to clarify who Allah is and what He really wants. Thus for us believers, the Quran is not only the pure untampered and eternal word of Allah, but is also the criteria and lens by which we judge whether something in another book is true or not.

4) BELIEF IN PROPHETS

Who are our role models, the men of Allah that received revelation and were divinely appointed to people to it and to each it to others both by their words and actions? Those are the Prophets (nabi is prophet and anbiya are prophets in Arabic) and Messengers (Rasool is a prophet and Rusul are prophets in Arabic) that Allah has chosen and sent.

Starting with Adam (AS) there have been thousands and thousands of Prophets sent to their communities throughout the ages. The chief among them besides Adam AS and Nuh (Noah AS) Ibraheem AS and those that came under his lineage. Just because doesn't mention Prophets from the lands of India or China or Europe or the American doesn't mean they didn't exist. Such prophets did come indeed but if all of the prophets the ones most great and most beloved by Allah and those especially blessed due to their forefather's great legacy of faith over those that came from the family of Ibraheem AS.

What do we know about this bless Prophet that Allah loved and blessed so much named Ibraheem?

The whole life of Ibraheem AS is a big testimony to the power of belief and faith. Here was a man who was not deemed significant by people during his lifetime. Yet Allah deemed him significant and love him so and let the world eventually know the great status he held with Him. Indeed in different portions of his life he was homeless or an exile or just a wanderer seeking asylum.

Ibraheem's AS life begins in the land of Ur, a city near the famous Euphrates river in the middle east. The gift that Ibraheem AS had was a highly rational mind, one that led him to utmost devotion and realization and deep friendship with the Lord of the heavens and earth himself. As he questioned society around him, he concluded that it was absurd to worship any other than the one Lord who created everything to existence and to whom belongs all our worship. When he come of age he devised a plot to show the people of his town their folly of worshipping the idol statues that they were worshipping.

Allah narrates:

"And certainly we bestowed Ibraheem with right-mindedness (in thought and conduct) in the past and certainly we are fully knowing about him.

He (Ibraheem AS) said to his father and his people, "What are these images that you are totally devoted to?"

They replied, "We found our fathers worshipping them (so that's why we worship him as well)". He (Ibraheem AS) said, "Certainly you and your forefathers are in plain error and misguided."

They said, "Have you brought us the truth or are you amongst those playing around?

He said, "Rather your Lord is the Lord of the heavens and the earth (so worship Him alone). He who created them (from nothing) and I am a witness to this (truth).

And by Allah I have a plan for your (false) idols often you go away and turn your backs!"

So (eventually when he executed his plan) he broke the idols to pieces leaving only the biggest one o that they may turn (and address themselves) too it.

(when they saw their idols, in shock) they said, "Who had done this to our gods? Certainly whoever did such is an oppressive criminal indeed!

(After some consultation, some of them) said, "We heard a

youth talking about him earlier who is called Ibraheem. They (collectively decided and) said, "Then bring him before the eyes of the people that they may bear witness."

(When he came before them) they said, "Are you the one that did this to our gods O Ibraheem?"

He (Ibraheem AS) said; "No, this was done by this biggest one here! Ask them (these broken idols) if they can even speak!

So they turned to themselves and said, "Surely you are the ones that have done the wrong and oppression (by worshipping these speechless idols). Then they were confounded with shame (and said); "you know full well that these (idols) don't speak!

(Ibraheem As) said, "Do you then worship besides Allah things that can neither bring you benefit nor harm?"

Fie upon you and upon the things that you worship besides Allah! Have you no sense?

They said, "Burn him and protect your gods if you are going to act!" (Yet when they threw Ibraheem in the great pit of fire) we said, O Fire! Be cool and safe for Ibraheem!"

Then they sought other plots against him, but we made them amongst the greatest losers (and spoiled all of their plots to thwart Ibraheem). And we delivered him and his nephew Lut (and directed them) to the land which we have blessed for the nations (the land of

Jerusalem and great Syria region). And we bestowed on him (Ibraheem), Ishaaq (Isaac) and as an additional gift, Ya'qub (Jacob, and all of them we made righteous. And we made them leaders, guiding (men) by Our Command, and we sent them inspiration to do good deeds, to establish regular prayers, and to practice regular charity and they were amongst the (true) worshippers (who worshipped and served us and us only)."

(Quran 21:51-73)

This is a beautiful passage in the Quran pregnant with many lessons for us. First we see how Ibraheem's faith is based on rationality and sound reason, logic he most powerfully demonstrates to the people when he executers his plot, when he gives his final blow of this argument of why they continue worshipping that which will bring them no benefit nor harm, they are left speechless and dumbfounded, knowing they are the wrong. Yet they were still in power, and instead of listening and following to Ibraheem's truth, they instead decide to kill and burn him so he is no longer threat to their ways and their power.

It is beautiful to see how strong-minded, how faithful, and how courageous Ibraheem is for Allah. Even when all of society and its influences were against him, he didn't budge. Majority of human beings, on the contrary, fall into wrong worship and a disobedient life that leads them to Hell due in a large part to the influence of other people around them.

Even the people around Ibraheem AS made and excuse of idol-worship being the way their forefathers also worshipped. They were basically saying to Ibraheem AS and to Allah, "Even if it doesn't make sense, this is the way we are used to, and we will stick to this way!"

Many of us fall into the same trap. We hang around people that don't take Allah seriously, that don't pray, that don't really live up to the beautiful standards of Islam, and thus eventually they rub off on us and our hearts get affected and we too fall into the same bad habits and actions. Indeed, many a times a Muslim living in the wrong way may even have moments of repentance where he (or she) wants to turn his life around, yet social and peer pressure from those around him makes him (or her) makes them lose their drive.

Just take a moment as you read this and reflect on how you yourself and your values and your beliefs and your life's decisions and your habits have been shaped by or directly influenced by the people and environment around you. The influence is greater than you think.

Ibraheem AS sets the gold standard that truth of Allah and His oneness, of life and the afterlife, of existence is what we need to base our lives around, even if the truth be totally against what our closest associates or family or society believe. Live and revolve your life around Allah, regardless of what other people think or say of you.

Ibraheem AS also teaches us how to wisely deal with those who don't believe in Islam. His own father was a mushrik (polytheist worshipping other than Allah) and sided with the community against his own son. Yet Ibraheem AS still tried to convince him to come back to the straight way, and even when his father wouldn't budge, said that he would still pray for him.

Many young people especially get so extremely passionate with Islam that then when they go through their major life changes to be move religions they start becoming very rigid and mean and harsh with their family and friends. They have to learn to be gentle with others as Ibraheem AS was with his father, to go slowly with others as they may not be at the same level as you in wanting to change their life. Humility is hard but essential for the spiritual seeker wishing to gain Allah's love.

His faith was so strong that Allah, the Lord of all of nature, commanded the very fire that they intended to burn him with to cool down for hi. They were dumbfounded as they witnessed such a miracle from the man of Allah before them. They still plotted against but in the end of the day, they failed and were the greatest of losers in this life and the next, while Ibraheem AS was blessed with his nephew Lut (Lot AS) becoming a Prophet as well as his two sons, Ismaeel AS and Ishaaq AS, the forefathers of two great nations. They were the loser in both lives and he was the winner in both lives.

If only they had listened to him!

All of these beliefs are essential for us to accept, yet they take on such a deeper flavor and awaken such a great power when they become the very reality we live our lives around, with unshakeable conviction of their truth. These Islamic tenets of beliefs that Ibraheem carried are the beliefs all prophets carried and lived by including Prophet E's (Jesus, son of Mary), as well as Prophet Muhammad (S) the final prophet sent to mankind.

5) BELIEF IN THE LAST DAY

We have thoroughly gone over the last Day, the Day of Judgement, as well as descriptions of Jannah (Paradise) and Jahannam (Hell) in previous chapters.

Believing in this article is a rejection of any other theory that humans have come up with like that of us reincarnating into different life forms on Earth, etc.

6) BELIEF IN DIVINE POWER AND DECREE

All things that have happened, that are happening and that will happen, in this life or the next, are all within the power and divine decree of Allah. In Allah's eyes it is all already written and said and done whereas in our perspective it is a reminder to be in total humility and surrender to the Lordship of Allah.

Believing in everything already being written doesn't make a real believer fatalistic, where

he gives up on any self-directed initiative of doing good, but rather makes a believer spiritually proactive, doing the best he can while in a spiritual awareness that in the bigger picture and in the deepest spiritual sense, it is Allah in total control.

We are ants in the ant farm of this world, beyond humbly submitting and obeying, how else can we approach the All-Mighty that created and sustains all the heavens and the earth and all realities and worlds?

As the poet said, the ant walking can't appreciate the beauty of the Persian carpet. Meaning that the ant sees only a red patch and then a green or yellow patch it's walking on, but only when we zoom out and look from our human eyes do we see how those same colors were put together to create the beautiful patterns of that Persian carpet.

In the same way, we may not understand a lot of the world's happenings especially when harm and suffering comes in our life, yet, we as believers know that it is the All-Knowing who is running the show and He operates with full wisdom that we rely on and trust, the beauty of which and the justice of which we will see and be explained on the final day.

Thus are the 6 essential truths that we Muslims believe about how reality works behind the scenes. Looked at another way the 6 articles set the stage for a pure transmission of the message and the heart of the message. We believe in (1) Allah and his oneness and that he sent (2) angels with (3) scriptures to (4) Prophets to warn about (5) the Last Day and afterlife beyond, with the revelation of the path to success of Islam as well as all happenings, good or bad, all being written and within (6) divine power and decree.

PRACTICAL BELIEF IN ALLAH's ONENESS

The true reality and what Islam preaches time and time again, is that Allah(God) is both above the system of the world's operations and in a sense is the system itself. Allah(God) is above the system in that He can manipulate the system and is in full control of the system, for example when he cooled off the blazing huge fire for Abraham (on him be peace) such that he had the time of his life there as is mentioned in our Islamic tradition. At the same time, Allah(God) is the system itself, even when *apparent* miracles are not happening. Even the regular doings, like fire itself burning wood like it regularly does, or nature, or any experience ever going on, is a sign of His Magnificence and Greatness.

The truth is, saying the physical and chemical laws are acting upon nature is actually us saying Allah(God) is acting upon nature. Or saying that nature has designed a system where there are observable physical and natural laws and patterns that govern the world, is in actuality us saying Allah designed the system where there would be such laws and patterns that govern realty.

And the doings of Allah emanate from the Spiritual Unseen reality which is in essence the true nature of even this apparently physical and chemical world. Thus we are living in more of a spiritual world than a physical and chemical one. WE LIVE IN A SPIRITUAL REALM! Think about that deeply, let it shatter all other concepts you have.

This is of course contrary to what our modern education system tells us, where the name Allah and the spiritual unseen is systematically uprooted from our heart, creating generations upon generations of Experiential kaafirs(those who deny His existence by the lack of awareness in their heart), even in Muslim lands. No concept of Allah in scientific phenomena of nature, means no concept of Allah whatsoever. The understanding of physical reality is stripped away from its spiritual essence, and without knowing that man too has a spirit and is not just made of flesh, man is lost in depression not knowing why he even exists.

The Godless Greek founding fathers and the ideological systems and educational systems that follow them are the greatest of the Pharaohs of human history.

More than just killing innocent babies and throwing people in concentration camps, they murdered our faith and experience in God, and what a greater tragedy can humanity have then being disconnected from our Source, our Sustainer and Intimate Companion, our Beginning and Final End!

PRACTICAL BELIEF IN THE ANGELS, the SCRIPTURES, and the PROPHETS

PRACTICAL BELIEF IN THE LAST DAY AND THE AFTERLIFE

PRACTICAL QADR is ACCEPTANCE AND SHUKR: "I AM CONTENT"

Accepting qadr on a deep level leads to a special spiritual fruit of total and radical acceptance of the present moment. Read this as a passage that you are reading to yourself, and feel the acceptance from within:

I am deeply and fully content with where I am in my life right now.

My value is not based on what I do and how young I do it at nor how much people appreciate me or how much they hate me nor how much change I bring to the world nor how impressive and full of achievements my resume is.

My value is based on Allah and how much He pardons me and loves me. How much He values me. That and that alone. His love for me and my love for Him, He alone is all I care about.

The people may judge. They may be disappointed. They may even appreciate

and celebrate. But it's all temporary when it comes to my relation to people. It's all not worthy enough to be too noted. Your job with them is to serve them and be with them and together with them connect back to Him, that is all. They are just one amongst the many ways, which take both private and public forms, of pleasing Him.

His judgement & His disappointment is alone something to worry about.

And His Love and appreciation and celebration is alone something to rejoice in even thinking about!

If He accepts us in that biggest day of ours where we meet Him,

definitely it will be a joyous thing, and that moment of gaining His salam and His love is single pointedly something to strive each moment in living towards.

I am deeply and fully happy with myself right now.

Every part of myself.

Every movement.

Every shine.

Every blemish.

Because I am here.

I am blessed.

I have Him.

I am willing to forget the rest.

And be content.

Day by day.

Year by year.

Slowly things will build.

So there is no reason for me to rush.

Long live Allah, the everlasting King!

Forever Lives Allah, the Truly Majestic!

I am Happy Knowing I Am Yours

KEY MINDSET SHIFTS BROUGHT BY THE QURAN

1. History and Identity

How we relate to our past determines how we relate to our present. You cannot be a fully solid community worker or a fully dedicated believer without knowing and appreciating your roots. This theme can be seen often in the Quran. The Prophet ﷺ before revelation was aware of his Arab roots and that he was from the descendants of Isma'eel, son of Ibraheem (AS).

Indeed the Arabs prided themselves in knowing their own lineage and ancestry, immediatlizing their heroes' lives and values they believe in and value (like truthfulness, courage, and generosity) through their lyrical poetry. The words they sung taught them who they were, preserving the identity of the tribe for generations to come. The Quran came in such an environment and swept away all other lyrics – it was now time for not another patriotic Arab to dictate who they were and what defined them. It was time for Allah, Lord of the heavens and of the Arabs and of all races to teach the Prophet ﷺ who they were and what values to honor and how to live by them. Glory be to Him and His perfect speech and expression!

Here are 3 ways that the Quran's message changed Arab identity, shifting them from the wild barbarians that were perceived as to becoming the greatest awakened spiritual, social, and political force at the time.

2. Heroes

The Arabs were proud of their heroes so much so that insulting them was like insulting their mothers and fathers. They identified ever deeper to those heroes who were a part of their ancestors and lineage. By knowing their own lineage, their tribe, and they could socially place where they fit like a GPS does for geographic location.

For example, we know the exact names of 13 of the ancestors of the Prophet: Muhammad son of Abdullah son of Abdul Muttalib son of Hashim son of Abd Manaf son of Qusayy son of Kliab son of Murrah son of Ka'b son of Lu'iyy son of Ghafib son of Fihr who eventually connects many generations earlier to the son of Isma'eel son of Ibraheem (AS). And among those ancestors of the Prophet (S), Ibraheem and Isma'eel (AS) were looked as heroes being the distant and ancient founders of the house, while people like Abdul Muttablib, Hashim Qusayy, and Fihr were known for their leadership qualities. The Arabs loved and praised those who were trustworthy and honest, those who were eloquent and expressed wisdom, those who were courageous in the battlefield even when feeling death and against all odd, and those who were generous and hospitable to their guests without fear of poverty. They were not a people that valued democratic participation as much as power through tribe and through following strong leadership.

In such an environment came the Prophet (S). The Quran celebrated some of their older cultural heroes like Ibraheem, Isma'eel, and Luqman (AS), but illuminating a different light on them all. That these men who were loved for their wisdom were indeed monotheists who lived and strived against all forms of idol worship and paganism, the very core of beliefs that the Arabs had misguidedly fallen into. Seen in this light, coming to Islam and worship of the One wasn't a coming to a newly invented faith but rather a returning back to the very roots of their ancestry.

And Allah even goes a step further and relates as scene so powerful in cultural implication never heard before that it leaves the Jews and Arabs in surprise and awe:

And remember Abraham and Isma'il raised the foundations of the House (With this prayer):

'Our Lord! Accept (this service) from us: For you art the All-Hearing, the All-knowing.

Our Lord! make of us Muslims, bowing to Thy (Will), and of our progeny a people Muslim, bowing to Thy (will); and show us our place for the celebration of (due) rites; and turn unto us (in Mercy); for you art the Oft-Returning, Most Merciful.

Our Lord! Send amongst them a Messenger of their own, who shall rehearse Thy Signs to them and instruct them in scripture and wisdom, and sanctify them: For you art the Exalted in Might, the Wise.'

And who turns away from the religion of Abraham but such as debase their souls with folly? Him We chose and rendered pure in this world: And he will be in the Hereafter in the ranks of the Righteous."

(Quran 2:127-130)

It was already known that Ibraheem (AS) built the Sacred House as the sacred relic they possessed of the rock that had his imprints on it confirmed. Yet here Allah was connecting their cultural source of pride, the Sacred House that they revere, as an establishment of not the idols and paganism but of monotheism. On top of that, in the passage Allah warps us back into time when the Sacred House was being worked on by Ibraheem (AS) and He reveals that this sagely ancestor had prayed for a Muslim nation to come from amongst his children and prayed for a messenger to be raised amongst them that would teach them and recite the verses to them and purify them – just as the house was Ibraheem's physical labor manifested, the Muslim nation now arising as nation and the Messenger Muhammad ﷺ coming from his progeny was Ibraheem's spiritual prayer manifested. This implied the Muslims were the true inheritors of the House and the spirit by which it was built.

Such an insight may seem small to us but was radical for the Arabs and the believers of the time. It gave the Muslims a deeper sense of meaning when they realized that they were following their forefather Ibraheem's (AS) footsteps that the Prophet ﷺ was restoring and furthering. It gave the believers context to their struggle: it is we as a people who fell off from the truth and fell into such idolatry and such immorality, and Islam is here to bring us back to the pure way and to give us Allah's pleasure and eternal dignity in this life and the next.

Besides Ibraheem (AS) and Isma'eel who they already celebrated as their ancestors and heroes, Islam gave the Arabs (and by default all of us), new and true heroes to look up to. Beyond the courage and generosity and truthfulness the Arabs honored, Allah introduced the uneducated Arabs to ab host of over 20 righteous Prophets along with other righteous people and being to look up to and respect and along with other evil and indecent people to look down on and whose actions (and sometimes existence to hate).

This is the passage that has the most of those heroes mentioned (18 to be exact) all mentioned in one place.

"It is those who believe and confuse not their beliefs with wrong - that are (truly) in security, for they are on (right) guidance."

That was the reasoning about Us, which We gave to Abraham (to use) against his people: We raise whom We will, degree after degree: for thy Lord is full of wisdom and knowledge.

We gave him Isaac and Jacob: all (three) guided: and before him, We guided Noah, and among his progeny, David, Solomon, Job, Joseph, Moses, and Aaron: thus do We reward those who do good:

And Zakariya and John, and Jesus and Elias: all in the ranks of the righteous:

And Isma'il and Elisha, and Jonas, and Lot: and to all We gave favour above the nations:

(To them) and to their fathers, and progeny and brethren: We chose them, and we guided them to a straight way.

This is the guidance of Allah. He giveth that guidance to whom He pleaseth, of His worshippers. If they were to join other gods with Him, all that they did would be vain for them.

These were the men to whom We gave the Book, and authority, and prophethood: if these (their descendants) reject them, Behold! We shall entrust their charge to a new people who reject them not.

Those were the (prophets) who received Allah's guidance: Copy the guidance they received; Say: "No reward for this do I ask of you: This is no less than a message for the nations."

(Quran 6: 82-90)

The enemies include Shaytan, the Pharaoh, the arrogant people who rejected or strove against their prophet and those who still try to do the same against Islam.

What made these heroes so great and different and these enemies so vile and ultimately hated and destroyed? What made these successful people truly successful that the other crowd just didn't have? It all starts with looking at how we define success.

REDEFINING SUCCESS

If you follow popular culture throughout human history, ultimate life success is defined differently for different people. Here are some of those life conclusions of what ultimate life success is determined:

- Those with the most money

- Those who benefitted the most people and made the biggest impact societally

- Those who are loved most and are all most popular with people

- Those who have had the most positive and diverse experiences.

- Those who had the most power

- Those who lived with deepest joy and life satisfaction.

- Those who lived most dutifully in taking care of and sometimes even dying for sake of their loved ones.

What Islam calls for is a total redefinition of what we deem as life success: not towards others but the one that lives most dutifully to Allah is the one most successful. He who enters

Paradise and is accepted in that close circle, is successful, he who is richest on the Day of Judgement and in the afterlife is successful, he who is most loved and celebrated on that Day is the one successful. The truly successful are not just those who are deemed successful in this life, but are those deemed by Allah as successful in the next life are the truly successful. And who are those such people? Those who believe and love and trust Allah deeply and are of good character with others and generous of their wealth and live righteously honoring the Divine Law and who are most conscious of and immersed in true Divine Presence, constantly praying and calling and mentioning Him – indeed they are the truly successful!

This thought and this redefining was not only mentioned once in the Quran but was mentioned constantly us to deeply engrain it in the hearts of the Prophet (S), the Companions, and us believers thereafter. It was this lesson compelled with the lesson of Allah's presence and trusting totally in Him that revolutionized their identities, their lives, and later the world. Allah and His truly guided people were once again on the center stage of the world, and it all started with the simplest of lessons unlocked of its power when truly believed and truly lived.

CULTURE & COMMUNITY

The close knit community and culture of love, righteousness, and beauty of Madinah was truly remarkable. Many a times visitors or even captives of war would witness the love for a few days and would be so affected that they would embrace the faith. Even as history unfolded, the Muslims had the wisdom to connect to the people at their level, embracing the good of their culture, guiding them from the bad of their culture and society, and after the essentials giving them license to express their Islam as they sought fit.

The shalwar kameez that the man wears in India and the thawb and sirwal that the Sandi man wears and the dish dasha that the Moroccan man wears are all different, but the heart is expressing the same beauty and truth of la ilaha ilAllah. The different clothes and colors of hijabs and abayas that Muslim women wear are beautifully different for they all express the unique expressions and the diversity that Islam embraces and has continued to embrace throughout the centuries. While the cloths may be different, they all embody the Islamic values of beauty, purity, modesty, dignity, and self-respect. They principles don't change, but he expressions can and do vary. The same can be seen in the diversity of Muslim architecture, food, languages, and cultures throughout the world.

In the process of globalization and as the world becomes ever more interconnected, there is more opportunity for different peoples to interact but there is also great risk of losing one's culture in the process. The logos of fast-food restaurants and global retailers have replaced traditional and local businesses who couldn't survive the onslaught of financial power of these chains. Ironically, in many countries the global chains are welcomed by the locals and prosperity and may see their own culture as inferior in the race towards "progress" the world is a part of. The solution is not easy but is not complete isolation from the world in attempting to preserve tradition and culture nor is it complete assimilation in attempts for progress and modernity and economic stability that leaves tradition and local culture behind. It requires a balance, and one that a group of scholars and the media and politicians and businessmen healthily come up with in both honoring the old while embracing the good of the new.

In many of our local communities, there is no sense of community. Of course this is a generic statement that isn't true at all communities, but it is true of many. But nowadays, the masjid has been reduced to a place of prayer and to hear scripture of the pulpit. This is not to say that these things should not happen in the masjid – of course they should – but the masjid in the time of the Prophet ﷺ was as much a community center of activity and constant interaction as it was a place of worship. People would sleep over there, would discuss personal matters like marriage there, resolve conflicts there, eat together there, wrestle there, and be a family there together.

Love must be in the hearts! For with love, the local communities transform into places of light where all are embraced and all feel comfortable being in like a fish does when in water.

In 1st world countries, Muslims are: (1) challenging current masjids to be more inclusive especially to women, youth, those of other faiths or those of other nationalities, (2) working to either make masjids more judgement free zones or to create 3rd spaces like spiritual centers or weekly meetings where people of different walks can come and happily socialize and easily spiritualize (3) doing cultural events like those in the arts or in the food space to celebrate the beauty and diversity of their culture (4) bringing in professional business management and business culture development instruction and seminars to the boards of local communities so they work more productively and of more integrity, and consciously build on awesome culture in their respective masjids and centers and the community beyond (5) working with a diversity of other organizations in the community celebrating together to bring about more impactful events and projects.

All of these are great efforts headed in the right direction.

KEEPING IT REAL

Now it's Your Turn:

1. Take some time out every week at least where you go over passages of Quran or Islamic lessons and refresh your iman and rekindle it.

2. If you find the means to go out and engage in conversations with those of other faith. When they ask you about Islam and you don't know something, research and get back with them.

3. Find scholars locally or virtually that you relate to and can follow and take as your mentors so you keep strong in your faith.

Reflection Questions:

1. Islam is the truth, yet how come Allah let so many other religions exist and where did those other religions go wrong?

2. What is the purpose of life and why are we here on this earth?

3. These articles of faith teach us what REALITY really is. Where do you stand in reflection to it?

SECTION 2:
THE PRACTICE

ISLAM: THE WAY OF SURRENDER

"You Alone we worship, You Alone we seek for help" the imam chants as he leads the men and women behind him in prayer. In the holy city of Makkah, five times a day, Muslims throughout the world, men and women, young and old, come together to worship and praise and glorify Allah. The masjid in Makkah has hundreds of thousands and up to millions of attendees at any given moment, and to see them all during the time of Salah (virtual prayer) standing, bowing, and prostrating before our Lord Most High all together as one body is a remarkable sight to see. The beauty and constancy of the prayer capture beautifully what Islam really is all about: to step into Allah's reality and then to give our hearts and our lives to Him totally.

This spiritual path, this way of life, this illuminated tradition that has survived and thrived all these centuries is all about surrender. Surrender your heart and your life to Allah and attain eternal peace! That's the invitation of Islam. Not only religiously, but even linguistically that is what the word Islam is associated with and what it means, surrender and peace. When two armies would be fighting and one finally surrendered so that a truce would be made and peace established in the land that was them surrendering to make peace in Arabic. In this sacred way of surrender that is Islam, we are called not to surrender to another creation, nor another army, nor even a holy man, but rather we are called to surrender and devote our lives to the One, the Creator of all and the One in need of need of no one. Allah Himself who else is Worthing of such honouring and praise? None but He for La Ilaha IlAllah, there is not divinity, no one worth of worship, except for Allah.

Men and women of all faiths and of all backgrounds come to the Prophet ﷺ to take his hand and embrace Islam. They knew what they were signing up for.

They were not joining a group of terrorizers, womanizers, robbers, plunderers or criminals or like what a lot of deceitful modern media may display Islam or Muslims as. Rather when embracing Islam, they were declaring we take you on Muhammad as our spiritual guide and leader and recognize you and bear witness that there is no god but Allah and that you are his final messenger! We believe in the revelation that was sent down to you and commit to living our lives in accordance with what Allah through His words of Quran and what you through your teachings as the emissary of Allah have commanded us.

> *"O you who believe! Respond to Allah and His Messenger*
> *when he calls you to that which gives you life! And know that*

Allah certainly comes in between a man and his heart and certainly He is the one to whom you all shall be gathered."

(Q 8:24)

This verse beautifully says how the way of Islam that Allah's messenger is calling us towards, which we detail further in this chapter, is the path to us gaining life. Here it's not talking about physical worldly life but rather spiritual life and eternal life in the High Gardens of Jannah. This verse was revealed when the call for defending the Muslims in war was being made, sand now many Muslims who like comfort didn't want to risk their life for the sake of their people. It was a test of faith and loyalty. Allah to remind the people and with His divine reframing, says that the Prophet ﷺ isn't calling you to that which will make you aimlessly make you lose your life but rather is calling you to things that will give you life! Would you like to gain the life of your dreams and live it eternally? This is the way! Do you want to feel true spiritual aliveness, freshness, depth, and close intimacy with the All-Loving? This is the way! Give your life in love and dedication totally to the Glorious who guided you to Islam and wants you to succeed!

And get sometimes the path many get harder and you may have a debate of whether you should follow your own desires or what Allah calls for, well in that case remember in the end of the day, you shall return back to Him for judgement, so choose the way that pleases Him most!

Even to the people of the book (the Jews and Christians), Allah says that a messenger has come now (the bless Prophet Muhammad S) with a clear revelation and the way of light so follow him:

"O people of the book! There has come to you Our Messenger, revealing to you much which you used to hide in the Book, and passing over much (that is now unnecessary or not commanded to this final community of Allah's). There has come to you from Allah a Light and a Scripture clear by which Allah guides whoever seeks His pleasure to the ways of Salam (peace, safety, surrender) and leads them out of the darkness into the light by His will and guides them to the well-established path."

(Q 5:15-16)

Just as the words of Allah are abundant with glorious praises of Himself, similarly Allah, like in the above verse, reminds us of the great status and position of Allah's Messenger Muhammad (S), the great stature of His very words of Quran that the Prophet ﷺ delivered and the stature of the noble path of Islam that the Prophet ﷺ called and lived as the best example of.

"Noooon, (A sacred Arabic letter and sound Allah begins with in this chapter). By the pen and what is recorded. You are not, by the grace of your Lord, mad or possessed (as your enemies foolishly and spitefully say). Rather certainly for you is a reward (waiting) without end! And certainly you have a character sublime and great! So soon shall you and they see who are the (actual) ones afflicted (with madness). Verily your Lord knows best who is lost on the path (of life) and who is guided (aright by Islam and living right and going in the right direction)."

(Quran 68: 1-7)

"So I swear by what you see and all that you do not see, (that) certainly there is speech of an honoured Messenger (who is delivering Allah's words). Not the words of a poet,

little of you do believe! Nor are they words of a madman, little of you do remember (how you considered him same all those years he lived with you, only now with this message you don't want to accept it so you call him mad)! (This speech is) revealed down from the Lord of the worlds! And had he (the Prophet) spoken other words (falsely as revelation), then we would have seized him by his right hand then we would have certainly cut off from him his artery (ending his life), and none of you would have able on to withhold him (from such). But indeed this is the message for the Allah-conscious (and not a false speech). And we certainly know there are amongst you those that reject, and certainly it is a cause of distress for the disbelievers. And indeed it sis the truth of assured certainty. So glorify the name of your Lord, Most High!"

(Quran 9: 38-52)

If there were any revels of forgetfulness of how much Allah loves and defends His Prophet ﷺ and His own words, the above passage consoles the hearts of our hearts as believers. The Prophet ﷺ is truthful these words are true, the Day of

Resurrection will indeed happen and we all shall be raised up before Allah and judged on our life accordingly no doubt!

"Alif Laaaaaam Ra! A Scripture we have revealed to you in order that you might lead mankind out from the depths of darkness into the light by the permission of their Lord, unto the way of the Exalted in Power, the Praiseworthy!"

(Quran 14:1)

So what are the practices of this way of light of Islam? Let's go over the 5 essential pillars of Islam first, then explore other commands Allah and His Messenger highlighted for us to follow.

THE 5 PILLARS OF ISLAM

Just like a house has its pillars without which nothing else can stand, so too does Islam have 5 pillars which server as the foundation for embracing and establishing the rest of the way of life that is Islam. The walls, the roof, the windows, and everything else are also important but without these pillars the rest can't be present or of true benefit.

1.   THE SHAHADAH

The shahadah is the simple two phrase testification of faith, which all the previous articles of faith were prefaced on.

It is to say with conviction, "I testify that there is no God except Allah and I testify that Muhammad is the Messenger of Allah."

By saying this simple phrase we are declaring the truth of Allah's oneness and the truth of Muhammad His Prophet, His final Messenger, and the way to Allah's pleasure and His Paradise. Thus contained within us saying this statement is belief in all that the Prophet ﷺ brought, taught, and commanded including all the articles of faith and all the words of Quran and the other pillars and obligations of Islam. The rest of the pillars are actions necessary for every Muslim.

2.   SALAH: THE RITUAL PRAYER

Five times a day at the very least Muslims are required to perform salah, or ritual prayer to Allah. It is one of the keys to entering Jannah and is one of the first things Allah will ask about on the Great Day. The Prophet ﷺ taught us how to wash up to prepare for prayer, which times in the day and night to pray, and how to perform the right movements and sacred phrases when doing the prayer.

"[Successful indeed are] those who guard their prayers".

(Quran23:9)

The full details of prayer and its rules are beyond the scope of this book, but suffice it to say that salah is life blood of faith for a believer, one who honors salah consistently and inside and one who neglect it or finds it burdensome has incompleteness in this faith and still has work to do to make his subconscious mind and desires to fully surrender to Lord Al-Mighty. It is our private meditative bonding time with our Beloved!

3.   ZAKAH (ANNUAL CHARITY)

As Muslims we are required to give at least 2.5% of our wealth in charity every year. If we give more than that the better for us, but as a pillar and obligation is the 2.5% known as Zakah.

Many scholars breakdown the responsibilities we have into 2 categories:

i.   Rights of Allah we have to fulfil and

ii.   Rights of others we have to fulfil for Allah's sake.

Salah is from the command of Allah and from the rights of Allah, while Zakah is from the command of Allah and among the rights of others we must fulfil. Some believers are focused so much on rituals like prayers and fasting but when it comes to charity or integrity or good character they are failing. Others have great character but don't care about prayer or fasting or the like. A true believer honors all of his/her duties with Allah and with people.

Charity helps us detach from the money we so covet and the life of this world we so obsess over, it helps us to give to those in need of it. It helps us to empathize and care for the well-being of others, and lastly but not leastly it is of our greatest meant of investing for the life hereafter.

> *"And establish the Salah (in your life) and give the Zakah and whatever from the good your send forth for yourselves, you shall find them (those good deeds) with Allah (on the day you meet him and as a meant of salvation). Certainly Allah is Ever-Watching of what you all are doing."*

> (Quran 2:110)

4. FASTING IN THE MONTH OF RAMADAN

As Muslims, we follow a lunar –cycle based calendar rather than a solar calendar especially for our religious days and holidays. The 9th month in the Islamic calendar is Ramadan, a blessed month where Allah commanded Muslim men and women to fast from dusk till sunset every day of the month. I call Ramadan the Muslim spiritual Olympics for it is that blessed month where the masjids are filled for prayer; where food after sunset is abundant, where even those Muslims that came out of the closet just for the month have a spiritual mindset along with everyone else.

> *"O you who believe! Fasting has been prescribed to you as it as prescribed to those before you so that you may be perfectively Allah-conscious. [It is prescribed] for a fixed number of days, but if any of you is ill or on a journey the number (of days should be made up) with days later.*

> *"For those who can afford it the expiation is feeding one poor person, and he who give gives more will benefit more*

and ultimately it's better if you can keep the fast if you but knew.

Ramadan is when the Quran was sent down (from the heavens) as a guide for mankind and as clear evidence from the guidance and as a criterion of good and bad. So whoever witnesses the month should fast it but if you are ill or travelling then made it up with days later. Allah intends ease for you and not hardship and wishes you to complete the prescribed days and to extol Allah's greatness for guiding you all and so that you all be grateful (for His gifts).

(Quran 2:183-185)

5.   THE GREAT PILGRIMAGE:
THE BLESSED HAJJ JOURNEY

Once in a lifetime a Muslim is required to go on a sacred pilgrimage to Makkah. In Makkah is the sacred masjid as well as the sacred and ancient house that Ibraheem AS raised up for Allah. Ibraheem AS made the call for people to come to pilgrimage there and established the practice as Allah commanded him to do, but unfortunately over the course of centuries the sacred house (known as the Ka'bah or black cubic structure raised by Ibraheem) and the sacred masjid (known as Masjid Al-Haraam) were turned from places that celebrated Allah's oneness and the purity of living for Him to places of idolatory where all kind of evil and likes were happening. That is until the chosen and final Prophet, Muhammad ﷺ descendant of Ibraheem AS came. The idols and pictures around the Ka'bah were removed and once again the greatness of Allah alone was celebrated. To this day, millions and millions of people gather every year at the specified dates to perform the sacred rites of the pilgrimage. People come back transformed and touched, energized to live the rest of their lives for their actual purpose- to serve and please their Creator.

> *"Hajj is in the well-known months, so whoever undertakes to fulfil that duty then let there be no obscenity nor any wickedness nor any arguing during the Hajj. Whatsoever good you do Allah knows it. And take provision for your journey and the best provision is Allah-consciousness. So be conscious of Me O people of intelligence!"*

(Quran2:197)

SUMMARY OF THE 5 PILLARS

The 5 pillars are the base of action, behind which are the base of our beliefs. There are 6 primary articles of faith we believe in, the soul of the metaphysical system we believe in and live in behind the 5 pillars and other actions we commit to. Those 6 articles of faith are:

1) Allah (and His Oneness)

2) Angels

3) Scriptures

4) Prophets

5) The Last Day (and afterlife beyond)

6) Divine Decree

Allah sent angels down (specifically archangel Jibraeel) with different scriptures to different Prophets all calling to worshipping Allah alone and living in a pure righteous way so as to succeed on the Last Day and have divine decree on your side. Everything good or bad happens by His will alone, and no one operates and no event happens except being under His total control. In His highest dimension perspective, all is already decreed and done! And it is our job to pray and strive and hope to be amongst His chosen servants who gain His pleasure and love and mercy!

Those are the essential beliefs we live by, and what are the essential duties we uphold in order to live a life pleasing to the Lord? That's what the 5 pillars of Islam are.

5 Pillars of Islam:

1) Testimony of faith

2) Ritual Prayer 5 times a day

3) Annual Zakah charity

4) Annual fasting in the month of Ramadan

5) Once in a lifetime performance of Hajj Pilgrimage

Firstly we testify our belief in Allah's oneness and the Prophet Muhammad's prophethood so we enter the brotherhood of Islam. Daily we humbly pray to Allah standing, bowing and prostrating at least 5 times a day in order to remember Him and praise Him and show Him that we truly do live to please Him. Annually, we give at least 2.5% of our wealth to the poor and we fast during the daytimes during the month of Ramadan. And at least once in our lifetime we go to a blessed Hajj Pilgrimage to Makkah, visiting the sacred sites there and fulfilling the rites of the Hajj. All this we do in the manner our Prophet ﷺ and the Prophet sent to all humanity taught, for he was the chosen one and the guide that leads us to the straight way.

Of course, if one cannot afford it or is simple, too poor then one is not obligated to give the Zakah charity nor obligated to go to Hajj, and similarly if one is physically not able to fast in Ramadan due to some sickness, it can be made up later if possible or if not then an expiation can be paid to the poor instead.

Allah gave us Islam because He wants us to succeed and He wants to make our life pure and easy for us, not hard and difficult.

KEEPING IT REAL

Now it's Your Turn:

1. Where is the status of your 5 daily prayers with Allah?

2. How much charity are you giving to the poor? Does it equate to at least 2.5% of your saved wealth?

3. When is Ramadan this year? How can you fast and make the most of it?

Reflection Questions:

1. Why is the shahadah the heart and most important pillar of Islam?

2. Why were the prayers directed to be performed at least 5 times a day? What are some of the benefits?

3. How can we work to make spiritual practices automatic habits in our lives?

QUALITIES OF A MUSLIM

Allah outlines some of the various qualities He loves in various places in the Quran, and if you wish to see all these qualities exemplified in one man, look no further than our Prophet S. Lets' review some those passages:

> *"If it were His will, He could destroy you, Oh mankind, and create another race; for He has power this to do. If any one desires a reward in this life, in Allah's (gift) is the reward (both) of this life and of the hereafter: for Allah is He that hears and sees(all things). O you who believe! stand out firmly for justice, as witnesses to Allah, even as against yourselves, or your parents, or your kin, and whether it be (against) rich or poor: for Allah can best protect both. Follow not the lusts (of your hearts), lest you swerve, and if you distort (justice) or decline to do justice,*

verily Allah is well- acquainted with all that you do. O you who believe! Believe in Allah and His Messenger, and the scripture which He has sent to His Messenger and the scripture which He sent to those before (him). Any who denies Allah, His angels, His Books, His Messenger., and the Day of Judgment, hath gone far, far astray.

(Quran 3:133-136)

"And the servants of ((Allah)) Most Gracious are those who walk on the earth in humility, and when the ignorant address them, they say, "Peace!"; Those who spend the night in adoration of their Lord prostrate and standing; Those who say, "Our Lord! avert from us the Wrath of Hell, for its Wrath is indeed an affliction grievous,- "Evil indeed is it as an abode, and as a place to rest in"; Those who, when they spend, are not extravagant and not niggardly, but hold a just (balance) between those (extremes); Those who invoke not, with Allah, any other god, nor slay such life as Allah has made sacred except for just cause, nor commit fornication; - and any that does this (not only) meets punishment. (But) the Penalty on the Day of Judgment will be doubled to him, and he will dwell therein in ignominy,- Unless he repents, believes, and works righteous deeds, for Allah will change the evil of such persons into good, and Allah is Oft-Forgiving, Most Merciful, And whoever repents and does good has truly turned to Allah with an (acceptable) conversion;- Those who witness no falsehood, and, if they pass by futility, they pass by it with honorable (avoidance); Those who, when they are admonished with the Signs of their Lord, droop not down at them as if they were deaf or blind; And those who pray, "Our Lord! Grant unto us

wives and offspring who will be the comfort of our eyes, and give us (the grace) to lead the righteous." Those are the ones who will be rewarded with the highest place in heaven, because of their patient constancy: therein shall they be met with salutations and peace, Dwelling therein;- how beautiful an abode and place of rest!

(Quran25: 63-76)

Truly man was created very impatient;- Fretful when evil touches him; And niggardly when good reaches him;- Not so those devoted to Prayer;- Those who remain steadfast to their prayer; And those in whose wealth is a recognised right. For the (needy) who asks and him who is prevented (for some reason from asking); And those who hold to the truth of the Day of Judgment; And those who fear the displeasure of their Lord,- For their Lord's displeasure is the opposite of Peace and Tranquillity;- And those who guard their chastity, Except with their wives and the (captives) whom their right hands possess,- for (then) they are not to be blamed, But those who trespass beyond this are transgressors;- And those who respect their trusts and covenants; And those who stand firm in their testimonies; And those who guard (the sacredness) of their worship;- Such will be the honoured ones in the Gardens (of Bliss).

(Quran 70: 19-35)

From these passages, we can see a life pattern of total surrender, stability, and deeply-grounded life purpose.

Sufficient are Allah's own words in setting the best ideals for us! May Allah make us among the righteous and His chosen elect!

AN OVERVIEW OF THE ISLAMIC PROHIBITIONS

When we look at the many descriptions of what Allah loves and what he hates through His own words and through the guidance of the Prophet (S), there are some key values and attitudes that show up as a pattern. These are values and attitudes that the Prophet ﷺ fully embodied in his own life. Indeed all the descriptions of qualities that Allah loved and has prised in His servants were most exemplified in the life and character of His most beloved Messenger Muhammad (S), and all of His prohibitions were most detested by the Messenger (S). He loved what Allah loved and hated what Allah hated and gave His life totally to Him.

Some of the key values of Islam that we hold in the highest of regards are:

1) **Honesty:** believing in this truth and living in truth with full integrity.

2) **Simplicity:** Not concerning ourselves with unnecessary distractions or complication but rather preferring a clearly directed life revolving around Allah and His pleasure and His Praise and what He wants.

3) **Purity:** Committing to having a pure heart and a pure life so we can have a pure book of deeds when we meet Allah.

4) **Selflessness:** Remembering and fulfilling our duties with Allah, His Messenger (S), our parents, our fellow believing family, and the rest of creation and being generous with our empathy, listening, time, money, and selves while fulfilling those duties.

5) **Discipline:** Being committed to the laws Allah has set using our will power and good company to ensuring we don't disobey Him but rather fight if our base desires to ensure we fully surrender to the Most High.

6) **Wholeness:** Living Islam with balance giving and balanced time to our hearts, our bodies, our wholesome and healthy spiritually, socially, physically, and as best we can in all key areas of life.

7) **Total humility:** Devotedness and full expression of servanthood and surrender to the divine will, all while being in utter and speechless awe of the Majesty of His Oneness and His Omni-Presence and our final return to Him. This deep humility fosters a sense of deep sincerity, gratitude, and love with All-listening and the Most-near.

Below I'd like to summarize key prohibitions extracted from both the words of Allah Himself as well as the Prophet traditions. Going over all the references would be too exhaustive as they are the focus of many other Islamic books. This list is meant to be a reminder to those who know and an exposure to those who don't know about the Islamic spiritual tradition along with these rules that help us embody and embrace the beautiful Islamic values including the seven we mentioned above. I've broken the list down by body parts following the framework that many scholars in the past have also used.

1.   THE HEART/MIND:

The role of the heart and mind is to harbor good thoughts and feelings that Allah is pleased with, steering away from those mental or emotional patterns of thought and feeling that can lead to the weakening of faith or the displeasure of Allah.

PRAISEWORTHY QUALITIES AND ACTIONS:

- **Humility:** Boosting yourself up while looking down or putting down on others.

- **Sincerity:** doing things purely for Allah's sake and making His pleasure our heart's and life's purpose.

- **Deep faith:** Believing in and having faith in the revelation of Allah and the words and way of the Messengerﷺ.

- Thinking good of Allah.

- Accepting His decree with all your heart.

- Accepting His commands with all your heart.

PROHIBITIONS ON QUALITIES AND ACTIONS:

- **Pride and Arrogance:** Boosting yourself up while looking down or putting down on others.

- **Insincerity and showing off:** Doing this for other than Allah's sake, for example praying and giving on charity just so people say you are righteous.

- **Having doubts about Allah:** The Prophet (S), the afterlife or revelation that the Prophet ﷺ changed.

- **Despairing of Allah's mercy and thinking:** There's no point in repenting or turning to Him thinking it's too late and that we've gone too far and there's no way He can forgive us.

- Feeling safe and completely guaranteed Allah's Mercy and guaranteed Jannah so we become complete in our duties of Allah.

- Unjustly or consistently thinking ill or suspiciously or negatively or hatefully against others.

- Desiring that which Allah deemed unlawful

- Not having regret for past offenses and disobediences that you did against Allah's commands.

- Jealousy and wishing others had less of the blessing they are experiencing not learning or attempting to learn the obligatory knowledge needed to practice your Islam.

2. PROHIBITIONS OF THE STOMACH

- Consuming prohibited food (like pork or dead carrion or meat that Allah's name isn't recited on) or prohibited drink (alcohol or other intoxicants or drugs).

- Consuming food you bought from haram earnings (like gambling, stealing, selling forbidden goods, or earnings on interest).

- Unrestrained lust and greed for food, money, women or any other objects or experiences of this life.

- Unrestrained anger especially whereby you hurt other unjustly

3. PROHIBITION OF THE TONGUE:

- Backbiting and talking ill behind one's back

- Mocking and talking ill to someone in their presence

- Talebearing and gossiping and even more so when it can lead to trouble and conflict the community.

- Lying

- Cursing

- To like about Allah or Islam or to speak without knowledge while claiming or acting as if you do have it. (Saying some statements like Allah having son or there being another Prophet after Muhammad ﷺ takes you out of the fold of Islam.

- Saying or claiming you have done something or accomplishment when in reality you haven't

- Swearing on Allah's name on things that aren't true.

- Accusing another at something without reason or without evidence or witness

- Bearing false testimony

- Lewd or sexual conversation with other than one's spouse.

- Reciting the Arabic in Salah or Quran improperly and without any attempt of learning the correct way of pronunciation.

- Joking or mocking righteous people of Allah

- Calling or inviting others to evil

- Speaking against Islam

- Producing music or vain talk especially one that has lewd conversation or cursing in it or calls to bad words or evil demonic symbols or demonic energy.

4.   PROHIBITIONS OF THE EAR:

- Listening to any of the above prohibition of the tongue

- Listening in on private conversation not meant for you.

5.   PROHIBITIONS OF THE HAND

- Killing unjustly

- Hurting unjustly

- Stealing

- Accepting bribes

- Gambling

- Hurting animals or other creation for no reason

- Writing things that are among the prohibition of the tongue and are unlawful

- Short selling someone

- Not paying someone his/her wages

- Not paying one's debts

- Earning money in haram ways (like selling haram food or lewd magazines or earnings of interest, etc.

- Spending money in disobedience and in haram prohibited things

- Using things or money you borrow for a certain reason for other than their intended purpose

6.   PROHIBITIONS OF THE EYES

- Looking at other uncovered or in general looking lustfully. (Be modest, polite, professional, and public in your gender interaction dealings.)

- Looking at those things private to others like in one's house or accounts for so.

- Looking and preferring the objects and experiences of this world over those of the afterlife.

- Believing and seeing only physical reality as real but denying the spiritual and unseen realm. (Disbelief in the unseen realm or in being like angels that dwell in that realm takes one out of the fold of this noble path).

7.   PROHIBITIONS OF THE PRIVATE PARTS

- To not be privately alone with a marriageable person as it may lead to temptation

- To be sexual with other than one's spouse (includes masturbation, homosexually, bestiality, etc.)

- Having anal sex or sex during your wife's period

- Being naked in front of an unmarried other or looking at nakedness of an unmarried other.

- Reciting Quran or attempting to pray Salah while in a state of sexual impurity

8.   PROHIBITIONS OF THE BODY

- Not fulfilling your Islamic obligations like prayer, fasting, zakah, hajj, etc.

- Sifting in the places of evil and where Allah is being disobeyed.

- Men wearing silk or gold cross-dressing or arrogantly trying to show off with fancy clothes while in public.

- Women wearing tight clothes or revealing-skin seductive clothes or with head uncovered while out in public or arrogantly trying to show off and put down on others by wearing fancy clothes.

- Tattooing or altering the body for no reason (like sex change surgeries, etc.)

- To hurt or cut off or not serve one's parents or even one's family for no Islamically valid reason.

- To be ungrateful and verbally or physically abusive to one's spouse.

- To unjustly put down belittle and discriminate especially doing so another, just for being part of a certain race or class or a certain gender.

- To not write one's will down especially if one has assets to distribute when one passes away.

- Sorcery or astrology or black magic (engaging in this takes out of the fold of Islam. We aren't talking about simple eye-illusion based magic tricks we are talking about individuals who engage in Pagan rituals and Pagan worshipping other than Allah spirits [evil jinns] in order to predict future events and / or cast spells to harm other individuals).

- Worshipping other than Allah or claiming or calling on another falsely believed to be divinity besides Him or alongside Hi. (This obviously takes you out of Islam).

- Consciously harming your body.

- Suicide and taking your own life away. (This takes one straight to the fire.)

Those are some of the Key Prohibitions! For some matters there are exceptions which by studying one can learn the details of. For example, speaking bad behind another's back is a sin, but if that person happens to be doing a harmful act to others, let's say lying and deceiving others to take their money, then it's a noble thing to warn others about that so they are not hurt. Another example is that one should not expose one's nakedness other to one's spouse but let's say someone having any doctor do a check-up for breast cancer or prostate cancer or getting treated for it so in this case there is a justifiable medical reason if one had to expose one's self. Islam is a universal and comprehensive way of life guiding us to the way to eternal success. Instead of using our heart and mind and body organs for unlawful, we are called to fill our existences and our perceptions and our lives with that which is wholesome, Allah-Pleasing, and pure.

THOSE IMMERSED IN BEAUTY

If a person has good fortune, he or she goes through a period of self-reflection where he or she starts the journey of prioritizing Islam as a high life priority. If the resolve keeps burning, one gets closer and closer to Allah and deeper and deeper in the faith. People start upholding the 5 daily prayers and the other laws of Islam, frequently the circles of Islamic learning more and more. All of this is noble and the path to Jannah for sure. But the Prophet ﷺ and the revelation sent to Him called us believers to not settle just with the bare minimum but to strive to reach higher depths of Islamic expression. A deeper exploration of those higher spirituals goals and ideals as well as some key concepts and insights of the process of how to get there is what this chapter is about.

THE STORIES OF SOME SPIRITUAL HEROES

Before we go into the key spiritual concepts of Islam, let's first explore some famous life stories of past heroes that were lights for others in their lives and that can serve as inspiration for us. Some the details of those in the past may be based on folk stories or imagination as some of these are cultural legends now but the overall stories are true and have held true.

Fudail, son of I'yaad, was a gang leader of highway robbers located in what is now modern day Iraq. From the outside most would look down at him if they knew all he was busy doing: robbing casually, drinking, and messing around with women he was not married to. He wasn't always like this and had grown up as a Muslim. But family and life trouble along with bad influencing friends led him to survive in the streets.

Fudail was one of those people that when he went into something he fully went into something. Thus he wasn't just content with a small robbery here and there that would allow him to survive, he instead grew into an elite group of robbers that would mass loot whole caravans. The years went by going deeper and deeper in that dark, disobedient, and self-oppressive life. Fortunately for Fudail, he was different from this other killing and robbing colleagues in that he still had a conscience telling him that he was in the wrong and had to mend his life. He tried every now and then but failed to completely change his life. For example, when Ramadan would come he would try to comeback to Islam yet every time he was around his bad-influencing friends and the girls that loved him he would once again fall back down in that sinful life again.

There's a story of a highway robber mentioned in spiritual circles that was probably about him or that at least is capturing one element of what was going through his mind. A caravan was passing through the roads and was then ambushed by a group of robbers. As the caravan travellers stood on the side on a hold up, the robbers rejoiced at the variety of elegant products, spices, and goods. One of the robbers offered another one some of the food they were looting. The robber declined the food and said he was fasting. One of the traveller got angry hearing hat and said, "Here you are sinning and stealing and plundering our goods yet you are pretending be righteous by fasting? What good is fasting for a man like you that's stealing?"

The other robbers got angry of the travellers tone yet this robber with a face of regret and humility replied, "This fasting is one of the few little things I do in comparison to all the evil, and yet I hope Allah bless this little good I do such that it takes over and pulls me out of all the evils." The traveller was silenced and shocked of such a saintly response. Later that traveller saw that very robber in religious clothing crying and repenting to Allah thousands of miles away in the Holy Masjid (mosque) of Makkah. The robbers hope and prayer was answered.

And so it was with Fudail. It was one of his nights off, where instead of robbing he would go out to see one of his favorite women. Along the way of going there, he heard a caravan traveling on the road nearby. He overheard them saying that they should break camp quickly before Fudail and his band find them there. Fudail laughed to himself of how famous he'd become that random people traveling even knew his name. But what he didn't realize was he would soon hear those powerful divine words that would hit him just in the right spot for him to completely turn his life around. A man in was beautifully reciting Surah Hadeed, the powerful Chapter 57 of the Quran.

The reciter went through verses that talked about hypocritical Muslims behave and how they'll be devoid of Allah's mercy on the Last Day. Fudail's heart was melting. The verses were speaking directly at him. As the words of Allah vibrated in his ears and humbled his heart, the tears started flowing down his eyes in regret and repentance. By the time the reciter recited the 16th verse where Fudail heard Allah's words of "Is it not time for the believers to humble their hearts in awe for the remembrance of Allah?" and it was over with. He had broken in tears of regret of. He had decided, it was time to break away from his past, run away from home, and start a new righteous life. And that's exactly what he did.

He got some leftover money and without even saying goodbye, left with another caravan while keeping his identity secret. Destination? Makkah. The land of the pilgrims and the righteous.

The perfect destination and environment for repentance was chosen, but now the real battle of self-purification and spiritual cleansing now began. In the first couple months, his will power was tested a lot. Struggling to readjust, temptations to go back and longing to reconnect with his old friends and loved ones came up. But Fudail persisted. The image and fear of him being sentenced to the Hell-fire for his misdeeds remained and propelled "O Allah, forgive me!" His pleas never ceased, neither in the day or night. He closely connected to righteous scholars, spiritual grants, and other seekers on the path. The temptations to steal, to kill, to lust women, and to drink, which were once temptation that his whole life revolved around, now became the most detested thing in his heart. How did such powerful transformations grow in his heart? For Fudail was now on a journey to please Allah. He gave his life for Hi. And once he realized that His beloved didn't like these lowly activities, he gave event the desires of them up. His spiritual teacher assisted him on this path. Once he realized the Most Loving loved people studying about Him, remembering Him, praying for Him, and giving in charity then those activities became exactly the things he committed to doing. As the years went by, Fudail's sincere repentance and his act of deep immersion paid off. In the circles of knowledge, he became a scholar with a specialization in the Quran and the saying of the Prophet (S). In spirituality, he became a spiritually realized master devoting his energies to daily hours of meditative remembrances and prayers. He would split his time living between the holy cities of Makkah and Madinah. So constant was his worshipping to Allah and so deep was the joy he would experience while worshipping and praying Salah that people titled him "The Worshipper of the two sacred cities." He eventually married one of the daughters of his close teachers, raised a beautiful family and died in peace and in deep hope that Allah would forgive him of his past and accept him as one of the believers entering Jannah. May Allah have mercy on him and honor him and all of us with Jannah.

Fudail represents one of millions and millions of people who throughout the ages have committed to the spiritual path and reached the ends of the journey. Not all of them had bad pasts like that of Fudail. Some like Imam Ghazali or Rumi, were already scholars of Islam busy praying and teaching and giving in charity, yet even so they found their spirituality was lacking, their prayers empty of deep meaning, and their heart too distracted by fame and status and social position. They desired a fix and Allah so blessed them in their own ways. Others, like Shaykh Ibn Ataillah and Sh. Ibn Qayyim, were blessed from a young age to be raised by spiritual masters, they side skipped all of the struggle of redirecting their lives as they already had their priorities set.

Eventually they too became masters in their own right guiding others to the path too. Let me briefly go over the lives of these four aforementioned men, as they represent some of the most famous men who transformed their lives and who most eloquently called others to do the same.

Imam Ghazali was a famous scholar of his time. His righteous mom had decided early on that her kids would be scholars of the faith. It turned out that her elder son, Muhammed Ghazali, would not only turn to be a scholar, but would turn to be one of the most famous spiritual guides of his time. He studied under the best of the best, Imam Juwayni, who was the imam in Makkah. Even at a young age, Ghazali showed his wits by publishing a book on Imam Juwayni's teaching yet reorganizing them effectively and summarizing them in a way even Imam Juwayni had not thought of before. As the years passed by, Imam Ghazali ascended on his career ladder. He would debate with other scholars in public events and became known as a great scholar and debater who shut his debaters down. Soon he became the principal of one of greatest universities in the Muslim world, a position usually reserved for those with senior age and position. Years went by along with his worldwide fame of him and his teachings. He felt empty inside and fearful Allah would punish him on the Big Day for his heartlessness. He kept thinking about resigning from his position but his heart hesitated. He felt he needed some free time alone to work on himself without all the responsibilities of this position. One day he woke up and had lost his voice. He took this as a sign from Allah for him to now quit and execute his plan. He made arrangements for his brother to take care of his family and then set off to Makkah for the great Pilgrimage (Hajj) as well as to find a spiritual community to settle in to work on himself. He found a teacher and resettled in the famous city of scholars and spiritual master, Damascus, Syria. He stayed there for 2 years with his teacher and other spiritual seekers and experienced self-realization, more depth in prayers, and had identity shift and committed his whole life to the living the spiritual path. He went back home especially out of missing his family. People were amazed by the changed, more humble, thoughtful, and selfless man he had become. Yet for him his journey was not over. He rejected offers to be a teacher or to resume his old position. He rejected offers for debates. He set up a meditation center instead. He continued refining himself for another 8 years. Then did he write his famous "Revival of the Knowledge of Islam" as well as other works that called people to embrace the spiritual path and to work tirelessly on beautifying themselves internally.

Rumi's story is a little similar but his expression was different. He was well-respected scholar of a stable standing too. That is, until he met this strange yet illuminating being by the name of Shams Tabrez. Shams wasn't a typical sober and highly educated spiritual master. He was more of a wandering eccentric master who lived life through his heart and who would just as easily say you have spiritual potential as he would say to another they are a fraud and empty without fear of judgement or what they'd react and do. Rumi full in deep love. This wasn't a type of love that a man may have for his soul mate girl that makes him feel certain ways, this was deeper. It was as if Shams's vast spirit grabbed and puled at his spirit, looking them eternally together to the path of eternal beauty. Without warning and with the special spiritual spark nor planted, Rumi slowly lost interest in teaching to the deep disappointment of his students. Each time Rumi sat with Shams, it felt like just the words and the presence of Shams led to deeper and deeper levels of Rumi's own internal illusions fading. The company was spiritual edifying. When the master Shams peered into Rumi's heart and felt that the true was right, then he left the town without notice and without telling Rumi or anyone where he was going. Rumi was devastated. He cried and he cried. He mourned. He wailed. No one could avail his loss or suffering.

Right then and there, where he mourned so much that he lost all hope in life, did the spiritual energy that was being built up all those months strike him like a thunderbolt. The light that Shams was internally was the light he was too, the light of Allah shining all things into manifestation. The lessons all came full circle. Shams left exactly for this reason, he knew by leaving at that point, Rumi could look deeper beyond the form that Shams was to the deeper reality of eternal love he was pointing to. And it worked.

The rest is history. Rumi wrote thousands of beautiful line on the spiritual path, on insights revealed to him on the deeper meanings of the Quran, and on the tremendous power of the true love that we are. To this day, he is one of the most quoted poets and spiritual masters of all time, quoted even by many non-Muslims and in many languages. Ghazali's words sound like a strict father admonishing you to prioritize your life by putting spirituality first and preparing for the Last Day. Rumi however sounds like a man melted in deep love with His beloved Allah who is inviting you as well to drop your illusions and join the caravan of divine love.

The life stories of Ibn Qayyim and Ibn Ataillah are less exciting. They simply found spiritual masters to follow early on (Sh. Ibn Taymiyyah as Ibn Qayyim's teacher and Sh. Abu Abass Al-Mursl as Ibn Ataillah's teacher), followed their instruction and reached high heights of inner beauty and refinement.

Now let us dive more deeper in some essential theory and practice of the Islamic spiritual path.

THE PATH OF TAZKIA

Allah in the Quran says:

"Successful indeed are the believers!"

(Q 23:1)

And He also says:

"Successful indeed are those who purify themselves."

(Q 87:14)

This implies that the believers that are successful reached such heights by undergoing a process of self-purification and their internal realities to clean up the ungratefulness, disbelief, and illusion within and to let the light of faith whine within.

The science that this has been called through the ages is Tazkia (based on the Quranic term which means purification), whereas others used the term Tasawwaf or Sufism to devote the Islamic spiritual sciences. One thing to quickly note is that throughout the ages there have always been Muslims following the influences of their own desires and non-Muslims in saying that they were spiritual and were Sufis but sing that as an excuse to not pray or fast (saying they were already realized which was the whole point of the rituals so they don't need to do it anymore) or maintaining other deviant practices or taking advantage of sincere seekers and profiting and making money off of their backs or maintaining a deep cult-like expression and saying a lot of made up stories to keep you followers hooked. We are not talking about such groups but are talking about the majority of spiritual seekers, those who have sound creed and theology and a sound practice of Islam and are aiming to live just to please Allah in accordance with the Quran and the Sunnah of the Prophet (S). Spiritual exemplars after the Salaf [the first 3 generations of Muslims known to have abundant righteousness] like Ibn Qayyim, Imam Ghazali, Ibn Ataillah, Rumi, and many other scholars and righteous men of our past.

Although we could list out dozens of objectives on the spiritual path, we can centralize of to 3 overarching goals we as Muslims have on our spiritual journey to Allah.

1) Experiencing Tawheed

2) Developing Refined Taqwa

3) Developing Refined Akhlaq

Let's thoroughly breakdown each.

1) EXPERIENCING TAWHEED

Whereas practicing tawheed, or oneness, on the level of worship is us worshipping Allah and Allah alone, on a spiritual level it is the extinguishing of your reality of yourself and the world and seeing Allah's presence and his light manifesting everything including yourself. People who awaken to this essential truth of existence experience a level of happiness, joy, openness, and energy that is truly indescribable. It is the state of total surrender of all your wants, dropping all internal arguments with the "Now moment," coming instead into compete silent and internal acceptance of what is completely and fully. This awakening has been called tawheed (oneness), Haqiqa (Reality), Fana (Extinction of the ego), baqa (subsistence in the awareness of the divine reality), waqf qalbi (the heart at rest constantly in remembrance of Allah's presence), and Khudi (the self). Rumi himself uses dozens of names to point to this nameless reality that we all essentially are sustained from. The inner silence, the inner pearl, and love are some of his name for it.

In modern terminology, especially in the English language, the most common word used is consciousness, the discovery of which people term enlightenment. This discovery is the one common thread that all spiritual traditions have with one another, and Zen Buddhism in particular revolves all of its beliefs and teachings around this. There are also throngs of New Age "Spiritual but not religious" people who through meditational practices or other "enlightened gurus" live to discover this fundamental nature of reality and of themselves. There is sufficient Sufi material on this subject but it modern self-help books on hope and consciousness speak to us better, there is no harm in reading them too. Just as we as Muslims can take counsel from a non-Muslim doctor when we are sick, if it helps us to understand clearer and experience it deeper, we can explore the words of those realized others even of other faiths, as long as we do so with extreme caution, knowing that fundamentally these individuals, even with their higher states in their inner world, have deviated from the path that Allah called all humanity for, the path of the Prophet ﷺ the path of discipline in rituals and conviction in the creed all while in states of utter and deep realization of the oneness and greatness of Him.

We as humans constantly long and desire for that which we think will give us eternal happiness. When younger we seek toys and think and feel that will give us happiness. Within a few weeks to a few months even that becomes old and we seek another toy. Then we sought popularity or other gadgets or things as teenagers thinking they'd make us whole. Yet lo and behold within a short time we felt bored and sought new experiences. Then as adults the same thing. The wise are those who see through the cycle and break free. The wise men break free from the delusion of their own mind-created ignorance by realizing what beneath it all is the nature of themselves and of all reality manifested. The wise are those who have truly liberated and released themselves from the shackles of the mind itself, freed themselves from the incessant pull of the senses, and severed the deep threads of attachment to the world and our won self-limiting Concepts. The wise drop their longing for everything else other than what is truly real even if it leads them to sacrifice all else. Thus he is constantly basking in the witnessing of Allah's presence and light while fully devoted and obedient following the way of the Prophet (S).

> *"Then whenever you turn surely you shall find the face (and countenances) of Allah".*

> (Quran2:14)

So how does one arrive at such a discovery? There are a couple of ways that those who are realized have outlined.

i. THE REMEMBRANCE OF ALLAH

Allah praises and commands us to remember Him constantly throughout the Quran. In fact even when Allah mentioned that the Prophet ﷺ is an excellent role model for us to follow, He described the Prophet ﷺ as one who remembers Allah most frequently, showing us how much Allah loves this state of remembrance and this trait.

There are different types of remembrances of Allah in our tradition.

The greatest of remembrances and sacred chants are the words of Allah Himself, revealed in the unadulterated and rhythmic manner they were as an honor to this community of the Prophet (S). Chanting the sacred words of Quran is called "Tilawah", or the "following of", the Quran. Not just anyone who knows how to read Arabic can recite the Quran properly for it was revealed with distinct sounds and rules that one must learn to master the recitation of the Quran and learn the sounds as they were revealed. The science of learning the proper way of doing the sacred chanting of Quran is called "Tajweed", which literally means "to make better", and one who is known to be a beautiful reciter of the words is usually given the title of "Qari". The messages and meanings themselves are profound, and even the sacred vehicle of the sound carrying the message is profound, spiritually healing, and mesmerizing. No doubt, the Prophet ﷺ himself as well as many pure and righteous themselves used the power of the sounds of Quran to heal some physical ailments completely and it is well-known and effectively proven that the Quran is powerful in exorcisms of removing jinns and their evil possessing of others or their other harms.

Another type of remembrance is the circumstantial kind of prayers of calling out on Allah. For example, the Prophet ﷺ would say certain prayers before he ate and after he slept, or before went to the bathroom and after he did. These type of calling-cut-to-Allah remembrances, although essential to our sacred tradition and highly recommended are not called "dhikr" or remembrance as much as they are called "dua'a" or "sacred invocation".

The 3rd type of dhikr is the one spiritual masters are referring to when talking about it as a sure path to realizing and experiencing tawheed or the oneness of Allah illuminating all of existence. This is where one will continuously repeat the same sacred chant with Allah's name over and over again. Usually the phrase "la ilaha ilAllah", there is no god but Allah, is used (as people like the spiritual master Sh. Abdul Qadir Jilani taught) whereas other master said even the name of Allah himself repeated frequently is sufficient (as people like Sh. Shahdhili of Africa or Sh. Ahmad Naqshbandi of India taught). And even though we know "Allah" is the sacred name of the creator that He Himself has chosen to be known by in this earthly realm as well as the angelic realm and other realms, He still has many names the repetitions repeating of which can also lead to self-realization. For example, in the Hindu tradition you'll find people who have chanted "Om" or "Krishna" or a variant thereof (like "Om Namah Shivaya" or "Hare Krishna") as sacred names of the creator, and the creative force of the universe that He is, also have attained realization. There is something very ancient and something very human and natural to chanting, a tradition that has healed for centuries on end.

The dhikr leads to liberation for as it vibrates inside of us, it breaks us loose from the superficial play of feelings and thoughts, pulling us deep into a presence that has always been there and that is present even here and now.

What is revealed thereafter is nothing short of sublime?

Even the calm grounded Ibn Ataillah point to this reality while in wonder and amazement:

"How can it be conceived that something veils Him while He is the One manifest in everything?

It is a marvel how being has manifested itself in nonbeing, and how the contingent has been established alongside of Him who possesses the attribute of Eternity!"

And Rumi said:

"Lord, the air smells good today, straight from the mysteries within the inner courts of Allah! A grace like new clothes thrown across the garden, free medicine for everybody!

The trees are in their prayer, the birds in praises, the first blue violets are kneeling.

Whatever came from being is caught up in Being, drunkenly forgetting the way back!"

Here Rumi captures his intense love and his powerlessness to the great Bing. He starts by talking about how the spiritual energy of that day, the air, smells good, leading him to a deeper opening of witnessing the unseen realm. It so palpably tasty as an experience and as a healing for him, he calls it a grace like getting new clothes or a healing medicine. Then as he sees the natural beauties around him, the trees, birds, and violets, he sees beneath the surface that they too are all drunk in wonder and love and amazement

Like him dancing and praising and kneeling to the divine, lost in the "beingness" or the oneness of the light of Allah emanating and pulsating through all of their existences.

And remembering Allah through constant repetition of the sacred invocation is one of the key ways for us to awaken to seeing these realities ourselves.

Ibn Ataillah says to those who are unmotivated to saying the invocation as well as the rest of us that we should keep pushing forward with it for "Perhaps He will take you from an invocation of forgetfulness to an invocation of vigilance, and from one with vigilance to one with presence of Allah, and from one with presence of Allah to One where everything but he invoked (Allah) is absent."

Here he outlines 4 different levels of remembrance and invocation:

1) **Forgetfulness**: This is where we all start, our mind is chattering too much and our faith and spiritual levels are too low such that while we are doing our remembrances our minds are busy elsewhere and our focus is clouded. Indeed for some the distractfullness is so bad that they can't even sit peacefully for more than a couple of minutes without fidgeting or getting up, and the mind is in such deep conflict that it can't been sitting in peace and concentration. You can test for yourself how long you can sit in simple silence with your eyes closed before you have to move.

2) **Vigilance:** This is where now you are move concentrated and present-minded while doing your remembrances. You may even tangibly feel calmer and more relaxed after

your sessions and you notice your cognitive abilities and spiritual senses are slowly lightening.

3) **With the presence of Allah:** This is when you start to dip into the witnessing of reality and of who you are, but the awareness comes and goes. Perhaps in your remembrances it's there, but when you walk away it's gone in your daily life. Or sometimes the awareness is constant but when someone rubs you the wrong way and you get angry or when you got to sleep and wake up then the illusions come back up and your depth and awareness of His presence is gone.

4) **Only Allah remains:** This is where all your illusions have been denatured and so you see clearly Allah's light emanating everything, and that you in a full sense are also from the same source, and in some strange way you were what you sought. This is where anywhere you go you are in the remembrance of Allah – He is all you see in the world. This witnessing is a goal. Allah grant us such purification and openings!

Although the goal of remembrance is to be in a state of constant love and remembrance, the benefits are numerous.

ii.	ACCEPTANCE AND GRATEFULNESS

A second way to experience realization is by complete acceptance of the present moment and complete surrender to the now. When you drop all you wants and ambitions and all desires and all that you wish were different in life and come to life and Allah's will with open arms then if you are fortunate this will create a gap in the mind's chatter creating an opening and if you are even more fortunate the turning of your awareness back to itself purely in that mind can and sometimes does lead to a dissolving of the egoic mind of illusion and to a realized awareness. Sometimes people have glimpses of this experience or the full transmission of it when a life tragedy like a death of a loved one happens and they let go of their mind-generated story of their life that is causing them pain for a moment. Another way sometimes may experience all of this is by being deeply grateful, overdosing your heart with such gratitude that dissolves all other desires and wants a complete to Allah "Thank You" to life and existence itself with a big smile on your face, seeing all as a blessing that you don't deserve. This is tapping into the power of the now, awakening the deep force of your own awareness that has always been here.

iii.   GOING AT THE CORE OF ANY EXPERIENCE

Let's say you're experiencing a moment of joy or even a moment of pain. Ask yourself, what is at the core of this experience? What is out the center of it? If you do this often enough and deep enough it can allow you to see that the feelings and states and experiences you have even those you may deem "good" or "bad" are all like clouds and are transient but behind them and a the core of them is an unchanging presence that stays constant regardless of experience.

If you were to train in sitting your mind to a complete stop and experience any moment completely and fully and directly, you would also come to witnessing the witnessor behind the scenes.

iv.   SELF-INQUIRY

This is the method that let to Imam Ghazali's realization. In his book "Deliverance from Error" he mentions how while meditating and alone in Syria, he was deeply desirous of knowing truth and knowing reality. He investigated and through logic deducted he couldn't rely on his senses to find the essential nature of reality, for the senses sometimes deceive us. For example, eyes may see and oasis in the desert but in reality it may just be a mirage and illusion. The eyes in that case saw what in physical reality was not real. He also figured in that reflective introspection and search that logic and thinking wasn't sufficient either for it too can deceive. Yes, logic can help you prove that 2+2=4 but for more complex things many a times people use logic and come to wrong conclusions and end up deceiving themselves. For example, the passionate trinity-believing Christian will use logical analysis to defend his misguided beliefs of Allah having a son and that every who is not a Christian will go to the fire, yet in reality Allah is One and he will go to the fire for ever claiming such a blasphemy against Allah. Thus logic was used but it let to the wrong conclusion. Imam Ghazali continued in this process till he himself went through a type of sadness and emptiness as he went on to distrusting his senses, his thoughts and his feelings in telling him who he was or what the nature of reality was. What remains? This perhaps one of the key questions he then asked that silenced his troubled mind and that led him to deep realization of the fundamental truth of himself and the universe.

As one non-Muslim spiritual guide eloquently explained on the explanation of self-inquiry.

"Self-inquiry is a spiritual investigation of the I that is perceived to be real – in other words, "me" and "my story." Spiritual investigation reveals that any entity separate from the totally of consciousness is a false perception. Spiritual investigation reveals self as limitless being, in truth unbound by any and all perceptions of bondage.

Circumstances rely on physical, mental, and emotional bodies for their perceived existence. How can circumstances be considered real when their components are recognized to be essentially non-existent?

Paradoxically, in exquisite irony, by recognizing the essential unreality of what has been perceived as reality, there is a momentous release of deep love and compassion for all that is perceived!

"By recognizing your essential nature to be that which is unchanging, the experience of life is totally altered. It is not altered by any attempt to alter, but by surrender to that unalterableness at the core of all guises and thought, emotion, and circumstance. It is not altered by the cultivation of love and compassion. Unimagined, unsentimental love is pulling one level deeper into this embrace through every experience.

When the answer to the question who am I? Is experienced directly, the truth at the core of all form, whether physical, mental, emotional, or circumstantial, is revealed. The core is eternally present, regardless of body, regardless of experience. The core is eternally present, regardless of body, regardless of experience. The core is the presence of being, regarding pure intelligence and joy itself." (You are that by Gangaji, 145-146)

So question like "who am I really?" or "If I'm not my body or senses or thoughts or feelings, then who am I?" or "How does the experiences of self-experience itself?" or "Who is aware of this thought/experience right now?" when asked constantly can lead to mind-openings where you can directly experience this moment and realize. Even if you use other techniques, this one helps you directly to let go of the false conceptions of self and world that you keep holding that hold you seek from realization, so it is an inquiry that just like chanting, can benefit seekers of any spiritual fate.

V.   SACRED PRESENCE OF A REALIZED BEING

This is the 5th and final way of realization and is perhaps one of the most important ways to such. A person that is basked in realization has a spiritual energy that rubs off on those seekers around him and that can be strong enough to drop someone into realization especially if the seeker is open enough to receive that blessing. Notice how all the masters mentioned earlier had spiritual guides they had attached themselves to. The probability of you realizing Allah's light present and refining your character is increased thousands of fold by you being in the tutelage of someone who has spent the years discovering and embodying the true depth and spirituality of Islam. Through psychology and neurology we know that if two people are walking together with deep trust and healthy communication to each other, both the pace of their walking as well as the rhythms of their very heart starts to and syncs together to become one pace. This is what spending time with Allah-loving people in general can do and what spending time with a master can do for you too very subconsciously and effortlessly at times it syncs your heart in witnessing Allah's presence, in living and loving Him and His prescribed way of life completely, and in joyously and confidently following the ultimate spiritual master, the umbrella of mercy sent by the All-Merciful Himself the Messenger of Allah ﷺ himself.

Rumi's life story is a case in point of how a master can pull you in wordlessly even, and being like a sun of depth, pull a receptive seeker's heart into his orbit and eventually swallow him into the light of purity and bliss. If a student receives the opening in the presence of the teacher, usually the spiritualist Muslim term this Fadhl (or Fayz, which means grace and abundance) or tawajjah (meaning the turning of the face, giving the imagery of the teacher turning his/her face towards you and sending spiritual energy your way allowing for an opening).

The examples in our tradition of those are countless. Shaikh Abdul Hakim Siyalkoti mentions how it wasn't till the blessing of tawajjah hit him from the great Indian master Shaikh Ahmed Sirhindi that his heart finally fell into the realm of true dhikr and remembrance and realization. The more recent Sh. Ahmad Alawi mentions how his teacher through the blessing of the dhikr and his energy field of presence led him to the witnessing. Even non-Muslim seekers testify to such. The famous and more recent Indian teacher, Maharaj, that is author of the book "I Am That," was famously known for his gift. People would visit him from different parts of the world in his little apartment. The way one visitor described the experience was that Maharaj would ask you about your life and where you live and other small talk while looking straight at you sending that energy. As the conversation would continue, the energy would start hitting and you'd begin to see the folly and silliness of your talking. Eventually the realization would come and the visitor would be silent, looking in amazement at what is now witnessed. Maharaj would only let people stay for 3 day yet usually by that time he would have one fall into witnessing reality. For some this was a permanent shift whereas for others it was a glimpse that now they knew was there and that they would have to go deeper to fully make permanent. What Maharaj was doing was sending that tawajjah energy there while conversing and it would allow the visitor to drop and let go and denature their own version of reality and instead fall into that grace and presence. Of course, experiencing the reality of tawheed is of no benefit without the beauty of believing in the Aqeedah and living the Shariah that the Prophet outlined for us.

THE RUH VS. THE NAFS

One key concept used throughout Islamic spiritual circle is the battle between the ruh (the spirit) and the nafs (egoic self). The ruh is the consciousness within us that we have been talking about; it is the life-giving force and awareness within us, the angelic part of us, sometimes translated as the spirit that we have within us. The nafs is the mind and egoic mind we've been talking about, the entity that always pushes us to arrogance and stresses our own self-importance and pulls us deeply in desires of worldly things and experiences. The ruh is our angelic self, the nafs is our animalistic and lower self, and both are constantly in battle.

The goal of Islamic spirituality is this two-fold:

1) To discover the presence of our ruh and live from that place of total surrender to Allah's will such that the heart and the nafs become "mutmainnah," a total rest and peace.

2) To train the nafs with love and discipline to loving that which Allah loves and hating that which Allah hates till the point where it becomes automatic and subconscious and one has refined character of expression and a pure and protected from evil and sin life.

Rituals like prayer and fasting especially are designed by default to purify our internal realities such that we ideally and eventually both internally and externally surrender to the Lord Most High.

Allah says about the ruh:

> *"They ask about the Ruh, say the Ruh is from the amr (command) of Your Lord: of the knowledge only little been revealed to you all."*

(Q 17:85)

Shah Waliullah, the spiritual master and great reformer, said that based on this verse there are 2 key realms of significance and importance for us as humans and that we are mix of. One is the a'lamul khalq [the realm of creation] which includes all physical entities and our bodies and everything in this realm has limits of time and space imposed on it. The second is a'lamul amr [the realm of divine command] and this is the realm where the divine decrees for all existence is present, where limits of time and space are not imposed, and this realm, which doesn't have many human words to really describe it since it is so otherworldly and transcendent is where are Ruhs are from. We are essentially body and spirit, worldly and other worldly, all at the same time and that, along with us recognizing this fact and wilfully obeying Allah, is what makes our existence so miraculous and Allah so joyous to reward us so handsomely in the next life. This explains why some people can have dreams of exact events happening in the future for that is a glimpse from the realm of amr and divine command where time is all together and the future is as if it's already done so can be seen. This also explains why people can meet other people, even those who have physically passed in their dreams. For their spirits are still alive and roaming in the realm of amr in ways we can't fully understand.

This also explains how angels themselves and even the Prophet ﷺ could travel across billions of light years across the heavens without our own earthly time moving even one second, for time is not a limit when roaming energetically through that realm.

And lastly this also explains why the Quran itself is so profound, for it was not only a revelation of Allah's light and presence and the ruh that any human can discover, but even move so they are the greatest of transmission of transcendent yet specific in meaning and in sound revelation from the Most High who runs and sustains all the realms. It is no surprise then that when the Prophet ﷺ received revelation from Allah delivered by the Chief of all angels and the Sacred Ruh that Jibraeel AS is that the Prophet's ﷺ body would become physically extremely heavy and he would enter into a deep spiritual place where it felt like bells were being rung from all directions. The human Prophet (S), the most enlightened of all men, the beloved of Allah, was in those moments pulled into the a'lam of amr and timelessness, and was receiving the great guiding and illuminating and uncreated words that the One chose for all humanity to hear, chants, and live by before we meet Him, most glorified is He!, face to face, light upon light is the blessing of that revelation on his blessed heart, and light upon light be upon the spirits that truly inherit the sacred words!

This verse on the Ruh was revealed when the Jews, in arrogance and in a spirit of challenging and undermining the Prophet (S), asked him 3 questions that they felt they could use to display their depth of knowledge and the Prophet's ﷺ ignorance. 2 questions were of a historic nature that only those in the inner circles of elite of those learned men in the Christian and Jewish knew about. The last question was on the ruh and the Jews here wanted to show off all the Kabbalah (spiritual tradition in Judaism) knowledge they had and the frameworks and concepts they created. Shockingly for the Jews, the Prophet (S), who was expected to finally be silenced and disproved as Prophet, instead proved the truth of His messengerhood when revelation came down and not only confirmed details that the Jews knew about but also told them vivid details about those events (for example, the fear-inspiring looks of the people of the cave as their dog slept at the entrance or how the leader known as master of the two horns was not only just but also led an initiative to build a wall to block of Y'ajuj and Ma'juj, Gog and Magog peoples) silencing the Jews and having the sincere ones among them convert to Islam knowing that such knowledge the unable to read Prophet could only have been given by the Lord of the universe himself, when it came to the Ruh, Allah scoffs at their self-proclaimed scholarly status by reminding them that they have been given only little in knowledge. This implies that even if we were to collect all the knowledge of the ruh and the spiritual realm, it would be but a trickle of a drop compared to Allah's knowledge of the matter. And the same is true for all domains of knowledge as well. Stay humble and do what your told for Allah knows all and you do not.

2)   TAQWA: ALLAH-CONSCIOUSNESS

So far we have gone through some stories of righteous people of our past that lived and faced the spiritual challenges we also face and succeeded in reaching lofty spiritual heights (of course we are speaking from our own human perspective, and only Allah knows and is the final judge of who will be forgiven and accepted and who will not). We also have gone through one of three essentials of the spiritual path of purification and illumination and surrender that we are on that we are going through.

It may seem from the experiencing tawheed section that realization is the only good of the path. This may falsely make it seem like the path is a static one where Allah is unmoving and just waiting for us to realize, but in reality every single man and woman has a relationship with a dynamic and constantly interacting-with-us Lord. He guides and pulls those He loves nearer to Him and His inner circle of elites, and He misguided and pushes the disobedient and arrogant that He hates away from the mercy and blessing of righteousness, light, and His friendship. One who has realized and has been refined with deep Prophetic and righteous mannerisms and an intimate relationship with Allah is known in the spiritual circles as a wali (friend) of Allah, and the group of the friends of Allah are known as the auliya. Both words are mentioned in the Quran.

"Allah is the wali (friend and protector) of those who believe, He leads them from the depths of darkness forth into light. As for those who disbelieve, the rebellions ones (evil shaytan jinns) are there Auliya (friends and patrons and protectors), they lead them from light into the depths of darkness. These are the people of the fire, to devell therein forever!"

(Quran 2:257)

"Behold! Verily the friends of Allah will have no fear on them or shall they ever grieved. They are the ones that believe and are dutifully Allah-conscious. For them are the glad tidings in the life of this world and the last life! No

> *change will there be in Allah's words. That is indeed a*
> *supreme attachment!"*

(Quran 10: 62-64)

Some may say that they are no real levels of believers, everyone either is one or isn't. But this isn't true. Just as the Prophets hold higher stations than regular believers or just like in the Prophet Muhammad's community those who were alive while he was alive and supported him hold a higher rank, in the same way Allah has some of His believing slaves that are nearer to Him and hold higher rank, and that is why the Prophet ﷺ told even Jannah has many levels and that the more righteous you are the higher in rank you can ascend. This can be seen in Allah's words too. For example, in Surah Waqi'ah (Chapter 56) Allah calls the Jannah-going righteous the "people of the right hand," yet also makes mention of a group above them too, the "ones racing for ahead" (in righteousness and deeds and Allah calls those group of people the "near ones" to Him, fully immersed and enveloped by His love and approval.

The message and call is clear: Allah's relationship with you and your standing with Him is what defines you eternally so don't just settle for bare minimum but rather fulfil Allah's rights He has over you and go all the way forward in this path, giving your life to please Him and to ascend the higher levels of the sacred Jannah gardens!

Let's go over some of the qualities that makes Allah love those "near ones" so much.

1.   WARA-VIGILANCE

Taqwa itself. A word used frequently in the Quran and is often Allah-consciousness or fear of Allah, comes from the root word that forms the word "wiqaayah" in Arabic, which literally means protection. To have taqwa of Allah is to therefore protect yourself than doing or even getting near that which may pull you into doing that which will disappoint Allah or anger Him. Wara is almost a near synonym, for it means hyper-vigilance and caution to make sure you don't do anything that displeases Allah.

Whereas eman, and faith are like the operating system of our minds, taqwa is the anti-virus protection that will keep the whole system healthy and safe. A person of taqwa is one who guards his 5 daily prayers, who walks away or speaks up when there is backbiting or evil in conversation by another, who lowers his gaze and tongue from these marriageable to him, who ensures that any meant he's eating is slaughtered correctly and halal (permissible), etc. A person of taqwa is working hard to make sure his senses and his thoughts to make them filled with Allah-pleasing movements and far away from Allah-displeasing movements.

Another way to look at the spiritual transformation that occurs is through equations.

At first, it's my wants and that's all. This is the life of most humans on the planet who don't even know or care about Allah's commands, they only care about their own desires and their own life.

Then you get to a level of awareness of Allah's commands and what He wants from you but you internally still prioritize your own selfish desires above anything.

$$\frac{Your\,wants}{Allah's\,wants}$$

Then when you reach significant milestones, Allah's commands and your meeting with Him totally dominates your life, subduing even those lower desires such that they aren't acted upon or are broken and emptied.

$$\frac{Allah's\,wants}{Your\,wants}$$

Lastly, you get so deep in that your desires are whatever He desires and there is nothing left in your self-image except that you are his servant living to please Him Allah's wants = Your wants. It doesn't have to go in this sequential order as sometime one dips into the path of loving Allah, forgetting about themselves and reaches the goal of living for Allah faster, if Allah so permits.

Lastly a person in this journey leaves to be self-accountable, grateful for the good he was able to do always reflective and repenting and quickly apologetic for any mess up or for the simple fact of not giving enough for the infinite praises and thanks that Allah deserves. A person of taqwa is not one who let his evil habits thrive and grow but kills them off quickly or breaks off the environment that is causing one to be tempted towards evil and towards distance from the Lord. But if the desires are left unchecked those very desires and evil habits and bad company become the very things that end up making a man experience eternal bankruptcy, destruction, and humiliation. May Allah protect us all.

2.   DEEP DEVOTION

Oh what love, what devotion, what selflessness the righteous display to Allah following the footsteps of the Prophet (S). Here are some of the key acts of devotion we can do.

SITTING IN CONTEMPLATION AND CALLING

We have talked about dhikr and how it is a greatly rewarding practice that can also heighten our awareness and make us witness the nature of reality. The Prophet ﷺ himself would spend hours in praising and calling Allah especially at night.

Dhikr is us mindfully and heartfully repeating sacred phrases. The most common prophetic ones are "la ilaha ilAllah" (there is no divinity except Allah, SubhanAllah (glorified is Allah), alhamdulillah (all praise and thanks be to Allah) and Allahu Akbar (Allah is the greatest).

Dua is when we call on Allah and ask Him for our needs, for Allah loves our begging him and He is the all-knowing, all-hearing, and the One who takes care of us. The 3 most common dua's that Allah teaches us and calls us to do in the Quran are to seek for guidance (Allahummahdina), to seek for forgiveness (Astaghfirullah), and to send prayers of divine honor and blessing on the Prophet (Allahumma sale a'la Muhammad). Beyond this, it's good to have a daily habit or habit after prayer to ask Allah for anything and everything in your heart and both good in this life and the next life. Keep speaking to Allah day and night, make Him your best friend!

RECITING THE QURAN

The Prophet ﷺ received the heavy weight and act of divine mercy that the Quran was and he taught it to His companions with enthusiasm. He told them that not only for each verse but even for each letter Allah would give one the reward of 10 good deeds us that He loves the act so much.

Allah is the Creator of the universe and his primary manifestation is love, goodness, and mercy. This is why Allah's

Prophet would say "Bismillahirahmaniraheem," in the name of Allah, the All-Merciful and Ever-Merciful before Merciful love is what He has chosen for Himself, and the Quran is one great expression of that mercy. The Quran is a reminder of the grander journey we are on and the one, the loving, that everything revolves around, it is a light for us to use as a means of guidance for our hearts and lives, and it is a special living miracle of the sacred eternal word revealed to the consciousness of humans at the heart of their earthly journey before their final return back homes and back to Him. The Quran is a reflection of the universe for both are expressed from the same source. This is why not only natural wonders that awakens us to realize the divine presence but also all the verses in the Quran are known by Allah as "ayaat," miraculous signs pointing to the Divine. And lastly the Quran is a preview of the intense reality of Judgement Day and a preview of what Allah will say to humans as He either grants eternal success or sentenced eternal damnation to each human being. It is the criteria of eternity, so let the wise listen and follow! It is a mercy in that respect too for it guides us in how to prepare and be ready for that day. Reciting the Quran is a sacred art the righteous have preserved for all these centuries, learning it from the tongue of a reciter who learned the sacred art of changing from his teacher in a chain of direct teachers that goes all the way back to the enlightened heart and heavenly tongue of the Prophet (S), who received revelation. The true inheritors of the Book were those who, following the Prophet's ﷺ example were pure and enlightened beings who experienced the divine wisdom directly touching their hearts. They not only knew but also experienced that these perfect words and sounds are afterwordly. They understood that chanting the sacred syllables was an offering to Allah for the well-being of themselves, the earth, and all its creatures. They knew that the human voice chanting the sacred words has a healing power that replenishes the universe outside as well as within, creating harmony, and keeping both universes healthy.

"Say: believe in it (the Quran) or not (it won't affect Allah and is only your loss). Those who were given knowledge beforehand when it is recited to them fall down on their faces in humble prostration, and they say "Glory to our Lord! Truly the promise of our Lord [of a new and final revelation coming] has been fulfilled!"

They fall down on their faces in tears and it (the words of Allah) increases their awe-filled humility (before Allah)."

(Quran 17: 107-109)

"Is the one whose heart Allah has opened up for Islam such that he has received enlightenment from Allah (like the unfortunate one whose heart aren't blessed with such)? Then woe be on those hears hardened against the remembrance of Allah! They are the ones plainly lost (and misguided and in error).

Allah has revealed the most bountiful of speech in it's a book form consistent and repeating (reminders). The skins of those who fear the might of their Lord tremble threat and their hearts do soften to the remembrance of Allah. That is the guidance of Allah! He guides whomever He wishes to guide, and as for those He leaves astray no guide can lead him back."

(Quran37: 22-2)

In the first Quran passage just quoted, Allah captures how the power of faith over powers in awe and humility those who recognize with their heart that surely this is from the Sacred One Himself. The scene pained through the passage is a powerful one. Here were men who studied the Jewish or Christian cannon of scriptures for a lifetime and awaited the day when Allah would communicate again with humanity as was predicted and prophesized in their scripture and by various prophets that came when these true believers hear or read the verses of Quran for the first time and forever thereafter, as believers and Muslim converts now, glorify Allah in deep gratitude that such a great divine intervention and the final scripture and guidance was revealed in their lifetime. They fall down on their faces constantly when hearing Allah's words, they start crying not out of pain but out of being spiritually mesmerized and enchanted and of being in awe-filled humility of reciting His words, and awe that keeps growing perpetually in their ears as Muslims as they recite and reflect on the heavenly words more and more.

In the second passage quoted we see the great love and status Allah gives to those He guides with this great Book, those he illuminates the insides of, those He expands the hearts for to receive the nobility of the high lofty and dignified way that is Islam. Could one who receives such a blessing be equal to the one who is deprived of such and lives in spiritual emptiness, sin, disbelief, darkness, foolishness, and misguidance? Of course not! One will be in Paradise and one will be in Hell! Then Allah praises His own words. They are the most beautiful of discourses and consistent in their message.

How does the true believer's heart respond to reading or hearing the words? The eyes well up, the hair and our ears stick up, and as Allah describes in this verse, the hearts and skin of the believer softens in awe and fear of the might of their Lord.

Such a spiritually induced yet physically palpable experience to Allah's words is what Allah calls His guidance, meaning He is the one guiding that heart to such beautiful experiences of true recognition and true listening and true following. Every time we ask Allah to guide us we are asking Allah to make us reach such a depth of belief so the following of the revelation thereafter becomes easy and effortless and automatic. Allah grant us such blessing!

SALAH: PRIVATE TIME WITH THE BELOVED

So quantity wise the first goal for us to establish the 5 daily prayers and after that we can increase to the daily Sunnah prayers if we wish to get extra blessings and after that we can start praying what is known as "Qiyam Layl," the late night prayers especially before the hours of Fajr. Quality wise we have two ideals: 1) to develop a love of the prayer till it genuinely becomes our joy and stress-reliever, 2) to develop and awareness of Allah's presence such that our hearts are in deep awe-filled humility during the prayers, a state that is called khushu'.

> *"Successful indeed are the believers! Those who in their prayers express deep awe-filled humility."*

> (Q 23: 1-2)

So what exactly is khushu', what I have been translating as awe-filled humility, and how does it differ from the spiritual state of the realization of tawheed and true dhikr we mentioned earlier?

Fortunately for us, Allah has defined khushu' for us in his revealed book already.

> *"And seek assistance (from Allah) through patience and prayer, and verily this is a big request except for the khashi'een (people of khushu').*
>
> *They are the one who are conscious/mindful that certainly they will meet their Lord and that to Him they shall surely return."*

(Q 2: 45-46)

So here Allah defines what makes these special hearts so filled with awe before Allah in their lives and most deeply expressed in their prayers. They sit down and have reflected on Allah's greatness and have a deeply engrained conviction that they shall soon meet their great Lord, and that conviction as it grows in their hearts naturally leads them to states of khushu'. Majority of Muslims, if they have ever heard a really powerful sermon on Allah's greatness and us meeting Him or that ever had listened to a powerful recitation of Quran especially in overpowered them and made them feel like Allah was directly in their presence and revealing the words to them have had a glimpse of this experience. Allah praises those who pure believers whose belief and trust in Allah and His words is so deep that that experience and state become a natural part and parcel of who they are.

How do we get there? Allah has answered that for us too, and He's done so in a passage we just recently went over! Can you guess? Yes, Quran chanting and reflection is the correct answer! When we repeat the sounds and reflect on their meanings and reflect especially on the fact that these are indeed the Creator of the universe's words themselves and that we indeed are going to return and be judged by Him, this practice leads us to heightened awe of Allah, and cleansing and soft and expansive light we can palpably feel in our hearts. And just like any meditational effort, to have it transform into a permanent shift of awareness and experience requires us to let go of the old "junk" within and the old outdated ways of being and experiencing and internally operating. For some, especially those of a soft sweet going-with-the-flow nature, the letting go usually happens much easier and faster and usually such a person can progress faster in the spiritual path. And of course, being in the company of or in the tutelage of those who are already there, especially if they are effective in teaching how to get there, can definitely help us shorten our time in traveling these inner distances within our heart.

On the Day of Judgement, Allah mentions how when all mankind is standing before Allah, every single person shall have khushu' and awe-inspired humility, which isn't hard to imagine considering the fact that Allah in all His might and glory will be right there as well as the frightening blazing monster of the Hell-fire and the expansive gardens of Jannah, destinations people, including you and we, are being sent according to our beliefs and how close or far away from Allah's path and revelation did we choose to live our lives. The test is not to have khushu' on that day when everyone automatically will, the test is to have it now even while we don't perceive these hidden realities. Allah grant us such deep faith and deep khushu'.

Now let us go through the sacred phrases, actions, and postures in the Salah itself, and some wisdoms or insights of why we do things the way we do. There are 4 main postures of our Salah: standing, bowing, prostrating, and sitting. And there are 3 main sections of Salah. Here I will go through the overarching things we say and do, while intentionally skipping over some details which can be found in any beginner's guide to Islam book.

We start by saying Allahuakbar (Allah is Greater (than anything and everything) while raising our hands and recite the first surah of the Quran, called Al-Fatiha or "The Opener," and then recite any surah of Quran. This is the first section of Salah.

Why do we say Allahuakbar? Why do we stand? Why do we recite Fatiha first? Why Quran thereafter?

We say Allahuakbar almost every time we transition from one posture to another for it is a reminder that despite our praises and despite our conception of Allah and despite our conception of what exists in totally out there, Allah is far greater. It is an expression of deeper recognition of His greatness, an expression of deeper humility as we realize that we are nothing in comparison to Him and how undeserving we are to be speaking to Him and on calling such greatness, and is also an expression of emptying all else within our hearts other than Him, putting Him above everything else and having our perception and our lives revolving around Him. Thus the believer, by "Nothing else is as great as you, all else fades away and is miniscule in comparison and is only in existence because it is sustained by You, so I turn to You and You alone in my calling and in my prayer and live only for You and Your Pleasure!"

After some small invocations,

> We start the prayer then by reciting the 7 verses of Al-Fatiha, the first surah in the Quran. The Fatiha itself is a special gift from Allah to the Prophet ﷺ and his community, a spiritually powerful prayer for guidance that defines our identity as Muslims who have

recognized, surrendered to, and seek guidance fro*m the Most High.*

(1)   All praises be to the Lord of the Worlds,

(2)   the All-Merciful, the Ever-Merciful,

(3)   the Owner of the Day of Recompense!

(4)   You alone we worship, you alone we seek the help of.

(5)   Guide us to the established way,

(6)   The way of those whom You have blessed (and smoothened the path for),

(7)   Not those who have invoked Anger upon themselves, nor those who have gone astray.

The first 3 verses are us praising Allah and calling on Him by His different names. All praises be to the Sustainer and Lord of the universe is us praising the One whose brought and is sustaining everything in the universe, the praising All-Loving and Ever-Loving is us praising the One who does all the sustaining and all of His doings out of love and mercy to His creation, not out of destruction or to wrongfully make them suffer, and praising the Owner and the King of the Day of Recompense and Repayment is us humbly praising the One who shall soon review our loan He gave us of life and see based on that whether our contemned existence will be of pleasure in Paradise or in horror in Hell. Our current and future existences are sustained and determined by Him, all praise and thanks to Him!

Realizing the great and central role that Allah plays in our lives, we show Him exclusivity and love and dedication, saying, "You alone we worship, You alone we ask for help." The One we pray to and the One we call to is You Alone, Oh Lord and Master of our destinies! Praising Him truly and expressing this exclusive dedication is what Allah loves and through the Fatiha and its repetition as a spiritual mantra and self-identity defining life philosophy, Allah is Himself teaching us the right words to say to win over His mercy and to attain eternal greatness and eternal nearness and eternal success in the eternal kingdom of the High Gardens of the Most High, whose greatness never withers and whose inhabitants' joy never ceases. We've established our humble position before Him, that we are His worshippers and His beggars and now we do our big ask. What do we ask for? Guidance!

For verily Allah says:

> *"… Then when the guidance comes to you from me then whoever follows the guidance no fear shall he have nor shall he grieve."*

(Q 2:38)

By asking for Allah to guide us we are asking to make us among those who live by what He revealed and what He is pleased with so we too are amongst those who will have no worries or fears in the life hereafter.

> *"Guide us to (and along) the straight way, the way of those whom you have graced"*

(Q 1:5)

Who are those graced ones?

Allah answers that in Surah 4 when He revealed:

> *"If we had ordered them to sacrifice their lives or to leave their homes, very few of them would have done it. But if*

they had done what they were actually told, it would have been best for them and would have been the greatest of things to strengthen them. And we would then have given them from our presence a great reward and we would have guide them further along the straight way. And all who obey Allah and the Messenger then they are amongst the company of those on whom is the grace of Allah – of the Prophets, the Sincere, the witnesses, and the Righteous, and what a beautiful fellowship they are amongst!"

(Q 4:66-67)

Allah here mentions four benefits of obedience: 1) being best for them, 2) establishing them in strength, 3) rewarding them and 4) guiding them. And He mentions 4 categories of people from highest to lowest rank included amongst those graced by Allah:

1) Prophets who were guides and examples appointed by Allah, chief of all of them being the Prophet Muhammad (S).

2) The sincere and truthful ones are the next in rank; these are those who have reached the highest depths of surrender and spiritual ranks and belief and obedience of their Prophet, who believe in him even if everyone else deems the Prophet a innate and who support fully the Prophet and call people to believing in him even if it cost their own lives and all their status and wealth. Abu Bakr (R) was the greatest of companions of the Prophet ﷺ and was given the title of Siddeeq, being amongst the sincere and truthful ones.

3)   Next are the witnesses to the truth, those who beloved and truly followed the way, including those who died and attained martyrdom for Allah's sake.

4)   Lastly, it is the large company of righteous people, the ordinary simple believers who did what Allah commanded and maintained their obligations before Allah.

So we ask Allah in the Fatihah to make us amongst this fellowship!

Then and lastly we pray to Allah to not make us among those who, despite receiving the guidance from Allah, knowingly fell off the path and earned Allah's wrath in this life and the next and also those who unknowingly fell off the path and will also be among the losers of the lost and misguided in the afterlife. The two very recent historic examples for such tragic failures are none other than the earlier two Abrahimic faiths, the Jews, many of whom openly and defiantly disobeyed Allah and the Christians, who foolishly started believing that Jesus (AS) is also divine and the son of Allah and that the law of Allah does not apply to them and thus unknowingly gave themselves to misguidance and to the fire.

And that's the Fatihah why does Allah love it so much that He made it necessary for us to recite it every cycle of prayer? There is special hidden blessing in it and they are just like right words Allah loves to hear. The Fatiha means the opener and the key for it is the opener to guidance and the key that unlocks Allah giving us guidance and love. Right after, we recite any passage of Quran we wish to recite in the prayer. Then we bow down and say Glorified is my Lord the Great.

Indeed we recite Quran hearing Allah's words while standing and recognizing the power and truth and so we then bow in awe and in that recognition.

"And certainly it is the truth of certainty so then glorify the name of Your Lord, the Great."

(Quran 69:52)

This is the second section of prayer where we praise and glorify Allah in 3 postures: the bowing, then standing, then the prostration. We stand and say that Allah listens to those who praise Him and we reply to that statement by saying Our Lord to You be all praise. Then we prostrate, putting our faces on the floor in a display of utter humility and surrender saying "glorified is my Lord, Most High." In our lowest of lows of physical postures we realize and glorify the one whose position and stature is the highest of the high. The final posture is the sitting where we do our final prayers before ending the prayer, we pray for eternal peace and security as well as prayers for divine recognition and acceptance and blessings on the Prophet ﷺ and also pray that we too along with the righteous servants all get eternal peace and security too. We also state that all good we do and all prayers we do is for Allah and say the testimony of faith, "I bear witness that there is no divinity except Allah and I bear witness that Muhammad is His servant and Messenger." And we end the prayer sending those around the globe.

My goal above was not to mention every detail of the prayer as that can be found in other books but to highlight some wisdoms of the form and phrases of the prayer. The prayer starts with Allah's words then continues with our praises of Him and end with our prayer for eternal peace and security.

Ultimately the Salah is a rehearsal of the Day of Judgement where we will stand together before Allah, the recitation are words of guidance we must live by, the praises make Allah happy to listen to us, and the ritual prayers are for us to be judged smoothly and be saved from the Hell-fire and admitted into the gardens, 5 of the prayers are the bare minimum for a believer to do daily so we are grounded in living this reality before the actual Great Day comes.

This whole book is about being inspired by the Quran and those who are truly inspired are mesmerized in prayers.

Salah is meant to be the highest life meaning development activity for the believers, for if done mindfully it actually grounds in our life's purpose of worshipping and meeting Allah, and it does this regardless of which life circumstance or time of life we are in. Truly in the beginning if usually does take some eman (faith) heavy-lifting to drop the illusions and attachments that distract us from prayer and to develop an affinity and love for it. We must learn to walk into the sacred context, for the Fatihah, the Quran, the Prayer are all invitations to living from and experiencing life from the sacred context. Thus the Salah done mindfully actually trains you to embrace the better and more truer and more nobler way to see Allah, yourself, life, and the world. Only by letting go of your previous baggage of your self-conceptions of Allah, and the world and yourself are you able to then walk into this new doorway of being, experiencing, and living in the world. And as you keep stepping into this context it can slowly become who you are, seeping deeper and deeper into your conscious until the sacred Quranic living context, the "glasses" of seeing the world through Allah's eyes as best we can, becomes your default context of being. In this way Salah, dhikr, I'badh, or any other right activity done with conscious effort and intention of living in context and doing it to serve and please Him actually become medicinal for you – they break your egoic motives for doing things and bring your heart close to living and moving and breathing for His pleasure's sake. This is what A'milusaalihaat, doing purifying deeds also means, engaging in those acts that are not only pure and scared and prophetic but also that help your conscious to let go of the sickness and delusion present inside you and to comeback instead melted in His glory and praise!

Thus we as believers know and realize, "there is no purpose of any life's existence except in serving You devotionally and seeking Your pleasure!"

UMMAH MUHAMMAD: THE PEOPLE OF SALAH

Throughout the world and even as we speak, there are a countless number of Muslims praying their Salah, all towards the direction of Makkah, all praying to the One and only God, Allah. This Salah is a gift that was given to previous nations including the Jews and Christians, but as Allah tells us they eventually followed their own vain desires and abandoned the prayers. They have deviated so far that now they even look at Muslims as strange when we perform our Salah prayers when indeed the very prophets they so revere did the exact same form of worship and called them to do the same!

It is inspiring to see the Sacred Masjid and the Ka'bah (cubical box-shaped structure that we pray in direction of) and all of the millions of people encircling it and praying there. It's a testimony to the inspiring fact that we as an ummah, as a nation, have spiritual world, in Makkah, the light of prayer continues to shine from there spreading all over the world. We are the people of Salah, the people that worship Allah the way He loves and accepts and has called all humans to worship Him.

Now coming back to our communal situation, although majority of Muslims do maintain the weekly congregational prayers of Friday Jummah prayers, the sad reality is that the majority of Muslims do not maintain their 5 daily prayers. I hope that by learning the importance of it and the wisdoms of it, if you are such a person not maintaining that obligation that you are now inspired to rekindle that spiritual and intimate connection with Allah, plugging in with private conversation in Salah with Him at least 5 times a day.

After the call to worship Him alone and rejection of the false idea of other divine beings, Salah and charity are the two commands Allah repeatedly mentions in the Quran like no other one. And remember how we just mentioned that Allah talked about how previous nations followed their desires and abandoned Salah? Well, Allah also mentioned now their final end will be like because of that, "fa yalqowna ghayya," then indeed will they face destruction! If you follow the example of the Prophet whom you love as well as the righteous and the guided, then you will pray following their lead in hopes that you will be accepted in Paradise with them. But if you or I keep the prayers as your last life priority, and die without ever having the habit of daily prayer let alone without ever experiencing the joy and high spiritual opening present, then it is feared that we too will in the end be sentenced like the previous people who did the some were – in after destruction of the fire.

Pray before you are prayed upon is a great slogan as a reminder and motivation too. What it's saying there is pray your daily 5 prayers before the unexpected moment comes when you die and your funeral prayers are prayed by others. After death everyone will want and hope to pray more or to be sent back to pray more, but by that time it will be too late. There are no returning flights back.

Allah also tells us about how when the angles go down to Hell and ask the people why they were in there, the 1st thing they inmates burning and moaning in pain fearfully and in after regret said was that they weren't among those people who used to pray their Salah.

Sufficient are these as reminders for those who really love Allah to establish the prayer in their lives! It's not hard, really. Just search and find out your local prayer times (there are even certain apps for this making your life easier), and when the times come in, go wash up for prayer and hit the prayer rug. It only takes around 10 minutes if we do it a little fast-paced, so 50 minutes total in the day for all 5. Is one hour out of 24 hours in the day too much for Your Creator to ask? It too much to ask for the One who lovingly created you and blessed you so much? The One that's been there with you in this journey along life all this time? The heart of faith replies of course, it's not too much, of course going to pray!" without hesitation.

Allah make us among the guided and amongst the true people of prayer, and may He save us from the fire and destruction and save us from actions that may lead us there, Ameen!

STANDING FOR PRAYER IN PUBLIC AND PRIVATE

Whenever Allah commands to prayer, he doesn't just say "Pray!" but rather uses the phrase "Stand up for the prayers." People stand up for what they believe in and what drives them and by us obeying the command and at the very least observing the 5 daily prayers, we are telling and showing Allah that we stand up for now other than You on Allah. It is a statement of loyalty, devotion, and commitment. As Malcolm, the Shaheed (martyr) of America, said, "He who stands for nothing will fall for everything." The true believer stands for Allah honourably. Yet majority of Muslims who don't pray or live their lives around their meeting with Allah are men and women who are confused, lost, and will fall for anything. Shaytan (the devil) takes the hearts of such people as playgrounds. Praying collectively has a powerful effect both spiritually and socially. Here the time for prayer comes and the real believers stop whatever they're doing and swarm like bees standing together in communion rehearsal for the day of judgement, for their you will also be standing together before Allah with all humanity, and in this life you stand in prayer so that in that day you hope you stand with them and the Jannah-entering community.

Whereas standing together in congregation can test and build how strong your awareness of Allah's presence is, it is the private prayers especially in the early hours before

Fajr prayer where intimacy and deeper sincerity and humility is developed. The last third of the night was highly emphasized time by the Prophet ﷺ for people to do their private night prayers and that is the time when he would stand for hours too.

> *"Is one who worship devoutly during the hours of the night prostrating himself or standing while taking heed of the (soon coming) Hereafter and hoping for the mercy of his Lord. (Like one who is empty and disconcerned from such effort and unbelieving of such realities)? Say are those who know equal to those who don't know? Certainly they are the ones (those who know and are so deeply devoted) who*

are (truly) reminded (by the power of revelation of the greatness of Allah and the greatness of the Hereafter)."

(Quran39:9)

"If only you could see when the guilty ones will bend low their heads before their Lord, (saying:) "Our Lord! We have seen and we have heard: Now then send us back (to the world): we will work righteously: for we do indeed (now) believe." If We had so willed, We could certainly have brought every soul its true guidance: but the Word from Me will come true, "I will fill Hell with Jinns and men all together." "Taste you then - for you forgot the Meeting of this Day of yours, and We too will forget you - taste you the Penalty of Eternity for your (evil) deeds!" Only those believe in Our Signs, who, when they are recited to them, fall down in adoration, and celebrate the praises of their Lord, nor are they (ever) puffed up with pride. Their limbs do forsake their beds of sleep, the while they call on their Lord, in Fear and Hope: and they spend (in charity) out of the sustenance which We have bestowed on them. Now no person knows what delights of the eye are kept hidden (in reserve) for them - as a reward for their (good) deeds. Is then the man who believes no better than the man who is rebellious and wicked? Not equal are they. For those who believe and do righteous deeds are Gardens as hospitable homes, for their (good) deeds. As to those who are rebellious and wicked, their abode will be the Fire: every time they wish to get away therefrom, they will be forced thereinto, and it will be said to them: "Taste you the Penalty of the Fire, the which you were wont to reject as false."

(Quran 32: 12-20)

DEVOTION CONCLUSION

Now I'd like conclude talking about devotion by recalling those images that warm my heart thinking about them.

The Prophet ﷺ would pray for hours every night and so his wife surprised by the constant devotion and love to His Lord asked why He ﷺ worshipped so much even though he was granted a station such that all of his previous and future sins were already forgiven. The Prophet ﷺ effortlessly replied, "Should I not be a grateful servant?" The Prophet ﷺ saw those devotionals as a way to give thanks to His Most Generous Lord, and He wanted to be the most grateful of servants.

There is also the story of deep gratitude of Abdullah ibn Muhammad, a student of the famous student of the Prophet (S), Ibn Abass:

Imam Al-Dhahabi mentions a story of one of the righteous men of the past- Abdullah ibn Muhammad. He got lost during one of his travels and ended up on a hillock. On the hillock he came across a tent. The tent was really battered, and torn all over, and there was a lot of wind blowing into the tent. So, the righteous man, Abdullah, peered in and saw a very old man. The man had no hands and was blind. On top of that, he was paralyzed. All he was saying as he sat there was: "All Praise is due to Allah who has preferred me (in blessings) to so many of His slaves." The righteous man, Abdullah ibn Muhammad came closer and put his head inside the tent. The man kept repeating the same dua over and over again. Abdullah said, "Assalamu alaykum." The old man asked, "Who is that?" Abdullah: "I am a traveller who got lost, but I have a question for you." Old man: "I will respond to your question, but you must do a favour for me." Abdullah agreed, and then asked,

"Why is it that I see you in this situation that you are in, that you are not able to walk, you do not have hands and you are blind. You do not have any wealth whatsoever, and you are thanking Allah for preferring you over so many of His slaves." Old man: "Do you not see that I am of sane mind?" Abdullah: "Yes." Old man: "How many of the slaves of Allah are insane?" Abdullah: "Many." Old man: "Then Alhamdulillah, (All Praise is due to Allah) who has preferred me over so many of His insane slaves. Do you not see that I am able to hear?" Abdullah: "Yes." Old man: "How many of the slaves of Allah are deaf?" Abdullah: "Many." Old man: "Then Alhamdulillah who has preferred me over so many of His deaf slaves." The man goes on and mentions about how he can still speak while so many of the slaves of Allah are mute. He goes on to mention of how he has been blessed with Islam while other people are worshipping idols, trees, humans, etc. Then Abdullah ibn Muhammad said, "You have spoken the truth. So what is the request that you have?" Old man: "All my family members have died. And the only one person I have is a small boy who brings food and helps me with everything as I cannot bring food or even feed myself. Yesterday the boy went out, and he hasn't come back until now. So please go out and find him for me." So Abdullah ibn Muhammad went out in search of the boy. After a period of time, he came on top of a hill. In the horizon he noticed vultures circling. Abdullah knew that vultures only circle around a dead body. Abdullah went to that area, and found the dead body of the small boy. A wolf had attacked him, killed him and eaten most of his body. Abdullah looked at the corpse and wondered, "How do I go back and tell this old man who has nothing in this world, that the only person he did have has been eaten by a wolf?" Abdullah thought of not going back to the old man, However, he couldn't bring himself to do that. So, he started making his way back to the old man and on the way, Abdullah remembered about the Prophet of Allah, Ayyub, alayhi salam. He entered the tent. Abdullah greeted him. Old man: "Where did you find him?" (He was very sure that the boy had been found.) Abdullah: "I will ask you a question first. Who is more beloved to Allah, you or His Prophet Ayyub?" Old man: "No doubt it is Prophet Ayyub." Abdullah: "Then who has had a more difficult test, you or His prophet Ayyub?" Old man: "No doubt His prophet Ayyub Abdullah: "Seek the reward then from Allah. I have found your boy on the top of the hill; the wolf had found him, attacked him, and eaten him." Old man: "La hawla wa laa quwwata illa billah. Inna lillahi wa inna ilayhi raajioon. Ash-shadu alla ilaha illa Allah." (There is no power or might except with Allah. Indeed to Allah we belong and to Him is our return. I testify that none is worthy of worship but Allah.) And the man kept repeating these phrases over and over again. He kept remembering Allah and then starting taking deep breaths. Abdullah felt as though the man would die. He picked up the man's head and kept giving him water. The man kept repeating Ash-shadu alla ilaha illa Allah, Inna lillahi wa inna ilayhi raajioon (I testify that none is worthy of worship but Allah. Indeed to Allah we belong and to Him is our return) until he finally died. Abdullah ibn Muhammad waited until he found a group of travellers along that valley. He asked their help in washing the body, wrapping it in the burial shroud and to dig a grave for that man. They buried the man and prayed Janazah over him. Abdullah thereafter went on in his journey. That night Abdullah ibn Muhammad saw the old man in a vision. The old man was looking good, seemingly in excellent health and condition. In the dream Abdullah conversed with the man. Abdullah: "How did you get to here? How did you become better? How did you change so much?" Old man: "My Lord entered me into paradise and it was said to me, 'Peace be unto you for what you have been patient upon, and what a good end you got.' That is the story of an old man. Someone whose name we do not know, who was hardly known, and who hardly had a life to live. And yet, one of the righteous men of our ummah was given a vision confirming his entry into paradise. He truly embodied the verse of the Quran, If you are thankful, then I will increase you. [Quran 14:7]

Once at the time of Hajj, there was a gathering in Mecca of some friends of Allah; amongst the youngest of whom was Junaid Baghdadi (ra). In that gathering, there was a discussion on the subject of 'Love for Allah' and as to who are the real lovers of Allah. Many of them expressed their views on the subject, but Junaid (ra) kept quiet. He was pressed to say something.

With his head bowed down and tears in his eyes, he said, "The lover of Allah is he who forgets his own self, remains engaged in Allah's remembrance with due regard to all its requirements; sees Allah with the eyes of his heart, which is burnt by the heat of Allah's fear; Allah's remembrance affects him like a cup of wine, he speaks the word of Allah as if All-Mighty Allah speaks through his mouth; if he moves, he does so under the command of Allah; he gets peace of mind only through the obedience of Allah; and when such a stage is reached, his eating, drinking, sleeping, awakening and, in short, all his actions are for the pleasure of Allah; he neither pays heed to the worldly customs, nor does he attach any importance to unfriendly criticism by people."

Imam Ahmad bin Hanbal Ra who was also known as Imam Hanbali, was a student of Imam Shafi'i. At the end of his life he told a story about going to Basrah. He narrated "When I arrived there, it was in Isha' time. I joined the congregational prayer in the mosque, my heart felt calm, then suddenly I wanted to rest." So he laid down. The masjid keeper came about and said what are you trying to do. Our great imam said he wants to rest and is a traveller. "You cannot do that, you cannot sleep in the mosque," came the reply.

The keeper did not know that the one he was talking to was Imam Ahmad, and Imam Ahmad did not introduce who he was. In Iraq, everyone knew who Imam Ahmad, a great ulama and expert in hadith, had memorized a million hadiths, very pious and *zuhud*.

At that time there were no cameras and social media technology like now, so people did not know his face, only his name that was already famous.

Imam Ahmad continued his story saying, "I was pushed around by the person told to get out of the mosque. After leaving the mosque, the mosque door was locked. Then I want to sleep on the terrace of the mosque. "

When he was lying on the terrace of the mosque, the keeper came again, this time angry at Imam Ahmad. "What else do you want, Shaykh?" Asked him.

"I want to sleep, I'm a traveler," Imam Ahmad answered.

Then the keeper said, "Not In the mosque, it is not permissible, on the terrace of the mosque it must also not be."

Imam Ahmad was expelled. He then said "I was pushed up to the streets".

Close to the mosque there was a bread seller in a small house functioned to making and selling bread. This bread seller was processing bread dough, while watching the incident of Imam Ahmad being pushed around by mosque keeper, the baker called from far away "Come Shaikh, you can stay at my place, I have a place, even though it's small."

He accepted the invitation. Imam entered his house, sat behind the baker who was making bread, still by not introducing who he was, only said as a traveler. This bread seller has a behavior that can be considered unique, if Imam Ahmad invites to speak, he answers. If not, he keeps making bread dough while reciting istighfar, *Astaghfirullah*.

When putting salt saying istighfar, breaking eggs with istighfar, mixing wheat, said istighfar. Always said *istighfar*.

Imam Ahmad continued to pay attention. Then Imam Ahmad asked "How long have you been doing this?"

The person replied "O, Shaykh, I have been doing it for almost forever. 30 years now. I have done this since then."

Imam Ahmad asked, "What is the result of your actions? (reciting istighfar)"

The person answered "Blessings. There is nothing I need but God will grant it to me. Everything I ask to God, is immediately granted ".

> The Prophet said "Whoever keeps istighfar, then Allah will make the way out for him from all problems and Allah will give *rizki* from ways he does not expect."

Then the person continued "All were granted by God except one, still one that God has not granted." Imam Ahmad was curious and then asked "What is that?"

The bread seller answered "I asked Allah to be met with Imam Ahmad bin Hanbal."

A moment later Imam Ahmad bin Hanbal said, "Allahu akbar, Allah has brought me far from Baghdad going to Basrah and even pushed by the mosque's keeper to the the road because of your *istighfar.* "

The seller of bread was shocked, praising Allah, apparently in front of him was Imam Ahmad bin Hanbal.

Ibn Masud (May Allah be pleased with him) reported: The Prophet (SAW) said to me, "Recite the Quran to me." I said: "O Messenger of Allah (SAW)! Shall I recite it to you when it was revealed to you?" He (SAW) said, "I like to hear it from others." Then I began to recite Surat An-Nisa'. When I reached the Ayah: 'How will it be when We shall bring a witness from every people and bring you as a witness against them?' (Q 4:41). (Having heard it) he said, "Enough! Enough!" When I looked at him, I found his eyes were overflowing with tears. [Al-Bukhari and Muslim Vol. 6, Book 60, Hadith 106].

Amongst some of the stories of the awliya, it is said that Imam Bukhari, Imam Abu Hanifah, and Imam Shafi'ee all read up to 60 Quran recitals in the month of Ramadan, reciting it day and night. When the recent scholar and spiritual master, *Sh. Zakeriyya Kandhelvi heard this he decided to attempt to do the same. MashaAllah an subhanAllah, Allah gave him tawfeeq to complete the reading of 56 Qurans in that one month.*

3. DEVELOPING AKHLAAQ – GOOD CHARACTER

The Prophet ﷺ had a magnetic heart-warming personality and rock-solid character and that was a part of why so many fell in love with him so easily, giving up their past lives and hearts' previous plans and desires and loves to now follow him.

"And certainly You have sublime lofty character."

(Quran 68:4)

Indeed He ﷺ saw his own role as to teach and train the people noble character with Allah, themselves, others, and the world.

Here then are some of the keys of us developing Prophetic character:

1.   KEEPING GOOD COMPANY

Is there anything more destructive to a human's fate other then another evil companion? How many husbands and wives have fell off by a bad-influencing spouse! How many people have lost their way because of their bad-influencing friends! The Prophet ﷺ gave a beautiful analogy that a righteous and good-influencing friend is like a perfume-seller, even if you don't buy anything and you just sit there some of the perfumes will touch and make you fragrant. And He ﷺ compared the bad-influencing evil friend to an iron smith, even if you don't make the tools with him, some of the dirt there will rub on your clothes. Here the Prophet ﷺ is teaching us the power of subconscious influences and how people can influence your heart without you even consciously realizing it, so choose to hang around good people, lest you too be influenced in the wrong direction and be destroyed.

2.   TRUTHFULNESS AND INTEGRITY

The Prophet ﷺ was known as "Al-Ameen," the trustworthy, even before his prophethood. It was a part of his DNA to be honest and just. Indeed one of the worst things you could offend someone by in the Arab culture at that time was by accusing him of being a liar. Usually we lie to either just bring some laugh or to make it seem like we have some knowledge or are in a higher position than we actually are. Allah especially hates when we say we did something that we never really did. Honesty can be uncomfortable at times but it's the best way to go – speak the truth or keep silent.

A big part of honesty and integrity is in dealings of money. Once the Prophet (S), in encouraging people to give their lives to defending the community, mentioned how if one is killed while fighting for Allah's sake and in protection of the community, then such a person is completely forgiven. Jibraeel (AS) who would come down sometimes to make corrections, came down and then the Prophet ﷺ added that the exception is for one who still has debts to be paid. Here a man has given his life for Allah's sake yet debts are so important in Allah's eyes to pay to others that ignoring them may block you from Allah's forgiveness! And so what is to say of the person who has debts to fraud, robbery, lies and deceit used to unrightfully take another's money?! How evil indeed are such people. My father once gave a big amount of money to a certain person so that a charity organization could be established to help poor people in that community. In sizing who he could trust, he chose someone whose family were almost like family friends, and who were religious such that some of the men would go out preaching and calling people to come to Allah and come to Islam. The family proximity nor the religious implications of stealing did not occur to that family member, for before we knew if the money was gone and the person disappeared and disconnected. This is the level of lonely behavior that many even so called "religious" Muslims are engaged in, Allah protect us. If you are paid for a certain service, do that service. If you are paid for a certain number of hours, do those hours to their full! If you loaned money for a certain project, use the money only for that project! Otherwise, prepare for a great Day of justice where the fraudulent will be with the other fraudulent in the blazing fire of Hell.

A person of true prophetic akhlaaq is someone you can trust, someone who has mastered his tongue and his hands to not use them in a way that's displeasing to Allah or unjustly hearing others.

3.   LOVE (FORGIVENESS, EMPATHY, DUTIFULNESS, AND PATIENCE)

Allah is All-Loving and once His love manifests itself on His servant, the servant becomes filled with love for others quite naturally. The opposite is also true, spread love to creation and the creator will love you too.

Love is what is so often missing in our interactions, in our families, and in our communities.

Love is the force that keeps a father and mother close to their children.

Love is the force that makes masjids and community centers feel welcoming.

Love is the force that makes communities work as one cohesive team.

Hate is the force that makes child fight with parent. Hate is the force that makes the environment even of spiritual centers and places of gathering poisonous. Hate is the force of us pulling each other's legs instead of encouraging success to one another.

Love or hate the - choice is ours.

Here are some keys to bringing more love in our lives.

4.   LISTENING AND UNDERSTANDING

Majority of all problems in relationships come from a lack of true listening and true understanding. Think about it. Can you think of one time where you had a conflict with someone else? Could the conflict have been prevented or at least handled better if there was better communication between you two? More probably than not you answered yes. Many of us spend so much of our time speaking our minds out, trying to get what we want, and demanding and trying to control others to fit our liking that we forget and become oblivious to the needs and wants of others. We forget they have needs and wants and their own feelings and thoughts too. This problem can especially be seen with failed parent – kid relationships, which are most common when the child is in their teen years. Let's use a father and son relationship as example. The father is well-meaning and yet feels like can't get the son in control and to focus on life's priorities. The son feels like he's doing the right thing and that dad just simply doesn't understand. They both end up continuously arguing and neither one is happy with the other.

How does one go about solving such a conflict? All it takes is one side to look at the problem differently and thus approach it differently, since usually such desire for an effective solution comes from the parent's side, let's focus on that.

The father must first learn to approach with empathy. Empathy ultimately means stepping out of your own shoes and perspective and instead step into another person's shoes and try to look at the world from their eyes. Instead of thinking that have is my son and how rebellions he is disobeying me and how ungrateful he is arguing with me, you'll think, "Here's my son, going through his own spell of emotions and trying to find his identity similar to how I tried to do the same when I was near his age." From this point of view you may be able to thus see how it's a fight for significance and you may also see new solutions you never saw before.

While communicating, seek first to understand. A good line to use right after son is done speaking is "Let me see if I understand you correctly," and then try to repeat what you heard in your own words. In this way, he can feel more understood and you can understand things better too. Sometimes kids just rebel for not feeling understood.

By stepping into those shoes, you may discover different ways to have son do what you in the end desire. It may work by someone else speaking to him, or by involving him in an extracurricular or a non-profit that helps those less fortunate, or by reconnecting to certain family members, or more extremely by even moving to another town so that the new friends there hopefully are better influencing. The skill of listening is universal, practice and master it!

B.   FORGIVENESS

Forgiveness is also an essential part of bringing love back in our lives, houses and communities. Allah has designed our lives such that we are surrounded by other people that can be just as imperfect, mistake-prone, and hurtful as we can be. And when we spend more and more time with people, hard feelings and arguments are bound to come up eventually. Accepting your own humanity as well of those of others and that we all prone to mistakes as we are is one of the first steps to being able to forgive others. Well, why would we even want to forgive another when we really deep down inside don't feel them deserving of being forgiven? We forgive others then for the wholesomeness of our own hearts. When we left that hurt and hate of another sit, it festers in our hearts and chains us down.

Allah gives us another motivation, which is He Himself forgiving us for our forgiving others.

Abu Bakr (R), one of the closest friends of the Prophet (S), was a very generous man who under-the-radar was giving money and support to his needy family members as well as many others as best he could.

In one of the greatest tribulations for his family, Abu Bakr's daughter Aishah (R), who was also married to the Prophet (S), was disrespectfully accused of indecency, false claim that Allah Himself cleared Aisha of. Unfortunately one of the accusers who mindlessly fell into the gossip happened to be one of the family relatives that Abu Bakr (R) was financially supporting. When Abu Bakr (R) found out, he cut off all the help he was sending his way. Allah revealed a part of a verse as a reply saying, "Do you not love that Allah forgive you all (by you forgive others)?

When Abu Bakr (R) heard these words he started crying, knowing Allah was also speaking to him to forgive his relative as his giving was a means of Allah forgiving him. Or course Abu Bakr would love Allah to forgive him! Without hesitation, he forgave and restarted the support.

The other two greatest classic examples of forgiveness for us to follow in our sacred tradition of Islam are the acts of forgiveness of Yusuf AS to his brothers and of the Prophet ﷺ to his tribe of Quraysh, both life stores which we have glossed over.

The Prophet Yusuf (AS) was just a young boy when his elder jealous brothers plotted against hi, throwing him in a well to be left to die and lying about his death. That left him cut off from his family, and because of that he was eventually sold as a slave and was also thrown in prison for many years. Eventually Allah turned the tables, making Yusuf (AS) the finance minister of Egypt while unexpectedly Yusuf's brothers, in dire poverty, came to him for help not knowing they were speaking to his brother, the one they abused and wronged so many years ago. Yusuf (AS), who could have easily expressed hate and revengefulness instead displayed magnanimity and forgiveness, forgiving them, expressing thanks to Allah for reuniting the family, and blessing him so, and generously providing for them thereafter. Many of us, had we been in the same situation, would have festered the hate all those years and expressed if when given the chance. Not Yusuf (AS). Similarly, the Prophet ﷺ also was abused verbally and physically by his very own family of the Quraysh tribe, who were his enemies. It got so bad that many of the weak Muslims were killed, many of the other weak Muslims fled to Africa for safety, and eventually all the rest of the Muslims migrated to Madinah with the Prophet ﷺ as things got so bad in Makkah. Yet a decade later when Allah blessed or tables to turn and the Prophet ﷺ entered Makkah as the new leader of the city, he could have chosen an eye for an eye, repaying back the harm that they gave him. Yet the Prophet ﷺ chose the path of Yusuf (AS) and forgave them completely even though the pain they gave him was very deep, for he was a man of Allah and knew that was the higher path. These are our role models who chose to forgive rather than to keep a vengeful heart, let us be true to them and follow their example!

Part of embracing the spirit of forgiveness is keeping in mind our desire for Allah's forgiveness and begging Him for it. It is no accident that usually those who are extremely repentant to Allah are also amongst the softest of hearts you'll ever meet. The true hearts among them have life's end clear in their mind, they know they will soon leave this earthly existence and they wish to leave without hurting others. When the spirit of forgiveness really engulfs a person's heart and becomes a part of who they are, you'll notice them sweating the small mishaps that happen in life, you'll see them in deep gratitude and feeling undeserving for what whatever blessings Allah has given them, you'll see them easily apologize and seek forgiveness from others when making any mistake, and you'll see them in deep humility both with Allah and with other people, not thinking themselves as self-righteous even though they spend constant hours in acts of devotion to Allah and acts of service to others for Allah's sake.

C.   SPENDING TIME TOGETHER AND FOCUSING ON THE LITTLE THINGS.

In relationships, the little things are the big things. A lot of times relationships, especially with parents or our spouse or with our kids, deteriorate simply because we don't spend quality time together. Not only does praying and fasting together build more of a togetherness feel in the home, but even things like walking out in nature together, reading something together, and going out together all foster deeper bonds. In a time where technology is ever-expanding, our artificial lives and friends on our screens something take away from those loved ones that are right around us. We have to schedule time where we unplug and reconnected to those we hold most dear.

Although the more adult companions remember all the community events that surrounded the Prophet's ﷺ life, it was the younger generation around the Prophet ﷺ that remembered the time he gave and how available he was to them in spine of his global concerns – the most. Aa'ishah (R), the young but very beloved wife of the Prophet (S), recalled countless events of the little things the Prophet ﷺ did that showed and expressed his love to her. She remembers with infatuation how the Prophet ﷺ raced with her early in their marriage and she was the victor and how years later they raced again yet this time the Prophet ﷺ was the victor. She remembers that day when the African entertainers were performing and how she rested her head on his shoulder so the rest of the community would see that public display of affection and know how close she was to the Prophet (S). Once Aisha (R) was narrating the gossip of the women about their husbands and how one woman in particular kept raving about her ex-husband was the sweetest, most loving, and most amazing of men that treated her amazingly and made her always sweep off her feet. The Prophet ﷺ lovingly remarked that he was to Aisha (R) as that man (Abu Zara'ah) was to his wife, except that he would never divorce her. The last Messenger of Allah (S), who had the heavy responsibility of receiving the final words of Allah and the responsibility to call all the rest of humanity to the accepted way of Islam and the worry of how his community would fare after his earthly departure and how they would fare on the Last Day before Allah, was essentially telling his wife Aisha (R), "You are my princess and mean the world to me, I love you and Allah loves you and I'm here to please you."

What I find most heart-warming about all of this is that many public figures in our day, Muslim and non-Muslim alike, have a public image of being of amazing character yet if people were to investigate deeper they would shockingly find that this person has secret slug he hides, as well as anger and a big ego that he unleashes on the weak ones in his home. For such figures, the more closer in his circle you get, the more dirt and evil and hidden abuse you'll find. The opposite was the case of the Prophet (S), not only were all the public and his community mesmerized and infatuated by him and ready to die for him (S), but also the closer you got to him the more you couldn't help but love him even more, and the more of his perfect character and unending love for Allah you would see. How wonderful and beautiful was our leader Muhammad (S), the chosen one who has stolen our hearts in love!

This is also why throughout the many years since the Prophet's ﷺ departure, even when hateful enemies of Islam came up with evil and false claims that Allah does not exist or that the Quran was man-made and not divinely revealed or that the Prophet ﷺ was a memorizer and a warmonger and a crazy madman, it was always the profoundness of truth of Allah's words as well as such beautiful character of the Prophet ﷺ that kept the community of the Prophet ﷺ for the most part by the intellectual and philosophical challenges brought by the deviant and lost ones. And this is why the opposite is also true, the more disconnected we are by Allah's words and to the Prophet ﷺ and his character and way of living, the more easily we are swayed away to lose our Islam and to embrace lies that our culture and community invites us to. The intention of writing this book was to be a spark that rekindles our awe for Allah's words, our love for the Prophet (S), our gratitude for being a Muslim, and our commitment to do better and be better as best we can in the noble spiritual path that is Islam. I hope that Allah has blessed your experience of this writing in closer achieving those goals.

Back to the noble character of the Prophet (S). As is a tradition that is still alive in the Indian subcontinent, many a times parents that revere a spiritual teacher and hope that their child gets blessed by their company will send their child to be a helper and an errand boy to assist in whatever the spiritual man needs. This was the case of Anas bin Maalik (R), who blessed as a young child to serve the Prophet (S). Anas (R) saw the Prophet's daily interactions with himself and with others and the more the observed him ﷺ the more he couldn't help but praise him. Anas (R) said that even though he served the Prophet ﷺ for 10 years straight (!), the Prophet ﷺ was so gentle that not once did he ever rebuke or scold Anas (R). Once the Prophet ﷺ asked Anas to do an errand for him and Anas (R) gladly accepted. But when Anas (R) went out in the streets he saw his friends playing and so he got distracted and started playing with them. A little while later, Anas felt the tap from behind, and his faced turned red in embarrassment. It was none other than the Prophet (S). When asked if Anas (R) had done the errand, the Prophet (S), who was the most empathetic and loving of people, understood. Anas (R) really thought he was going to get a scolding that day from the man he loved most, just like his parents or any other adult in his life would have done in that situation. Instead all Anas (R) got was the Prophet's ﷺ gentleness, who smiled and said not a single word to hurt or embarrass him. He ﷺ understood the frailty of human beings, he ﷺ never unnecessarily scolded or hurt anyone. It is no surprise then that usually whenever Anas (R) would narrate an experience he had with the Prophet ﷺ or a saying of his that he remembered, Anas would preface it by lovingly saying things like he was the most generous of people or he was the most beautiful in character before he would continue narrating.

One of the Jewish couples in Madinah, although they had not get converted, also recognized the Prophet's ﷺ great spiritual stature and wanted their child to be blessed by such grace. So a non-Muslim Jewish boy was also serving the Prophet ﷺ for a while! Unfortunately an epidemic of sickness broke out and the boy was one of those who fell ill. The Prophet ﷺ went out and visited the boy and his family at their home.

The boy was young of age but intelligent of mind. He realized that he was breathing of his last breaths. He also had already realized from the beautiful character of the Prophet ﷺ from the faithful and righteous community he ﷺ established, from the powerful heavenly words that were recited in his home and next door at the masjid, and from the praises of his parents about him ﷺ that he was indeed the Last messenger of Allah, wanting to be with the Prophet ﷺ perpetually and even after his death, he asked his parents for permission and then converted to Islam in the presence of the Prophet (S). A little while later he breathed his last and with a smile on his face returned to His Lord. I have always wondered what act the Prophet ﷺ could have done such that even the boy that witnessed his days at home and in the community could so easily want to convert and be one of his people and his followers. I have no doubt in my mind that it was not only the deep spiritual presence but also the little things in relationships like spending time and looking out for others that affected him most deeply.

Don't forget the little things, they are what matter most in our relationships! Giving time to others, actually listening to them and figuring out what they love and enjoy, showing them that you love them both with actions and with words, helping them while they are in need are all amongst the things which mean the most to people, and when done for Allah's pleasure's sake, will mean the most to us in the afterlife. Those who have the best of character will be closest to the Prophet ﷺ in the afterlife.

5. BEING DUTIFUL

A big part of living love is prioritizing high the duties that others have on you. Of course the highest duties we have to Allah and His Messenger (S), of loving, obeying, and defending them. After Allah and His Messenger, the ones who have most rights over us are our parents.

Allah says:

> *"Your Lord has declared that you worship none except Him alone and that you display beautiful character with your parents."*

(Quran 17:23)

Look at the great stature Allah gives to parents! In this verse, after the first universal command to not worship any other than Him, what is the next He deemed most important to be mentioned right alongside the great duty to Him? Dutifulness to our parents! Now in social interactions, Allah sometimes calls us to interact with "ma'ruf" which is agreeable goodness and kindness without harming the other. For example, this is the call Allah gives to spouses if they are divorcing. Don't yell and scream and be hurtful, but even while separation, do so with ma'ruf never forgetting that ultimately your journey is with Him. With parents the word used is not ma'ruf, but rather the Arabic word "ihsaan". What does ihsaan mean? Ihsaan is connected to the root words Ehat mean to beautify and to make something good and excellent. Whereas ma'ruf is you maintaining courtesy without harm, ihsaan is you displaying excellent and beautiful character, going out of your way to be the person and do whatever will please the other person. Going the extra mile to please them, that's the spirit and attitude that Allah teaches us to have with our parents. This was, of course, also reflected in the Prophet's ﷺ teachings and guidance to his followers. Overwhelmingly, the Prophet ﷺ usually always sided with the parents for he ﷺ palpably knew the great esteem Allah held that bond us. Once a man complained about his dad taking some money from him, and the Prophet ﷺ displayed some anger at his spirit of complaining and said that he (the man) and his wealth belonged to his father! In some other instances, men would come to join the Prophet ﷺ in defending the community in war or to join him in his pilgrimage. Even if they were expressing how excited and grateful they were for joining, if they said something along the times of they travelled a long distance and let their moms at home, the Prophet ﷺ would many a times send them back. In the Prophet's ﷺ eyes, although noble was the effort they were coming out for, service to their parents, especially their mothers, was a higher priority. Of course he didn't do with every companion, connotating that he perhaps was doing so to people he sensed that were neglecting their Allah – given duty to their parents. Regardless, the position they have in Allah's eyes is very high. Let us continue the verse having ihsaan with our parents, for it highlights more of the spirit we need to have with them.

"Your Lord has declared that you worship none but Him and that you are display ihsaan character with your parents.

Whatever one or both of them attain old age in your life, say not to them even a single word of contempt nro repel them, but address them with words of honor.

And out of merciful love, lower to them the wing of humility and say: "My Lord! Bestow on them Your merciful love just as they did when nurturing me in childhood!

Your Lord knows best what is in your hearts, whatever you do good deeds of righteousness, verily He is the most forgiving to those who turn to Him again and again (in true devotion)."

(Quran14:23-25)

Three other commands dignifying your parents are given here:

1) Speaking to them with dignity not saying even a word that could hurt them.

2) For the second command Allah uses and image of tenderness. Just as the bird extends its wing to its children out of motherly love and protection, so too should you extend your "wings" of support to your parents in love and humility.

3) And lastly, Allah commands us and reminds us to keep our parents in our prayer giving us one beautiful prayer for us to recite. Just as our parents nurtured us with love when we were young and weak, Oh Allah bestow your love and ease on them now as now they are getting old and weak.

As we grow older and stronger in our life getting busy raising our own families, it's very easy for us to forget giving due time and love to our parents who would love us unconditionally regardless. This is why our deen (way of life) stresses the rights our parents have so much, for even if no one in the community knows about our private relationship with our parents and even if our parents don't demand it, they still have great rights over us that true spiritual speakers must never forget as they journey on their path to pleasing Allah.

Perhaps the greatest example of the high rank that dutifulness to your parents can get you is that of Owais Al-Qarnee. He lived in Yemen, south of the Prophet ﷺ in the Arabian Peninsula. When he heard of the Prophet ﷺ and his message, he immediately converted and wholeheartedly accepted the teaching. And as the years went by, he had a burning desire to meet his spiritual leader and master, yet he dutifully kept taking care of his aging mother who needed him by his side. His spiritual rank ascended such in Allah's rank that the angels started talking about him to the Prophet (S). The Prophet ﷺ was spiritually informed that Owais wouldn't meet up with the Prophet ﷺ in this life time, but would get the opportunity to visit Madinah later on when Umar (R), the close friend and famous companion of the Prophet (S), would be leading the community.

Now Umar (R) was already an established member of the community and one of those that the Prophet ﷺ himself guaranteed Paradise to who was famous for his strict righteousness and his walking with dignity with his Islam and for many supernatural miracles that Allah gave him throughout his life. Yet here the Prophet ﷺ told Umar (R) that when this man named Owais comes to Madinah, ask him to seek Allah's forgiveness for you! Usually people would go to those they deemed more closer to Allah to seek their prayers for them. So people would go to the Prophet ﷺ or later to Umar (R) to ask them to pray to Allah for their needs and for forgiveness and blessing. But here the Prophet ﷺ is telling the very Umar (R) that people would crowd around and still refer to as a symbol of righteousness to seek prayers from this hidden unknown man that had never physically met the Prophet (S). That's the great stature the reached and the proximity to Allah he was blessed with for being so loyal to Allah and His Messenger and in being so dutiful and serving to his mother. It's so heart-warming and inspirational to hear of Owais (R) for it shows us how there are many hidden friends of Allah that many will never recognize us such that Allah so deeply loves for mastering the basics and for being as loyal and dutiful. Allah make us like them!

TEACHERS

Next in line of those we must honor and be respectful to are our teachers, especially those who are teaching us Islam. The true righteous scholars are the inheritors of the Prophet (S), for they carry on the knowledge and legacy and practices that the Prophet ﷺ left for us and guide others to do the same. Being punctual in their classes, writing what they say, and speaking or asking questions or leaving the class only when permission is given are all part of the adab that our traditional circles of learning teach and inculcate in the human being. Imam Shafi'ee, the famous scholar and sheikh and with the truly royal bloodline of being a descendant of the Prophet (S), said when he was studying under his teacher Imam Malik, he would even be cautious on carefully flipping his back pages as to not even in the slightest disturb his teacher while he was teaching. That's adab. In today's time when information is so readily available and manners even for the educated have faded away, it's essential for us to embrace humility and embrace the culture of respect that started from the Prophet ﷺ and his circle with his companions to circles of sacred learning and spiritual development throughout the Muslim world that have lasted and spread throughout the centuries.

YOUR SPOUSE

The first step in creating an Allah-centered home is having an Allah-centered marriage. If you are single, that means doing your homework before you say yes. You want to marry some you feel that you have chemistry with, someone that you feel you can healthily communicate and build a stable life and family with, and that you feel you can grow closer to Allah with. We're looking for our Jannah mates, people that we hope will increase our faith and righteousness and happiness in this life and that we pray will be means for us to both go together in the gardens of Paradise. How many men and women have been broken emotionally and spiritually because of their bad marriage! And how many have been empowered and transformed to heights by their blessed marriage!

In Islam, the primary role of financially providing for the spouse and kids falls on the husband, while the primary role of emotionally providing nurturing love and education falls on the wife, and both have a responsibility to preserve each other's dignity. All the character traits that we have mentioned earlier apply to us with our spouse and kids as well, and sometimes they are most tested in our very home.

We must especially be careful of misusing our tongues and hands in marriage, for any and all misuse will still come up on the day of judgement as a regret and embarrassment for us. Allah is still with us even when we are forgetful of His watch over us. The strongest of marriage in our community are those that are Allah-based, where both spouses have great character, spend effort in investing in each other's happiness, have healthy communication and healthy conflict resolution skills, and where they both make healthy decisions that lead to better life advancement and afterlife advancement for the whole family. They work as a team and are happy and faithful together. The 3 most common reasons for divorce are financial instability, toxic communication between each other, or emotionally getting more and more distant from each other. If divorce is the decision taken, one should maintain dignity and character and part with as much respect as can be maintained.

CHILDREN

The duty of parenthood is a naturally demanding one indeed. Beyond providing for them and guiding them to make healthy career and relationship and life decisions, we must effort our best to inculcate healthy Islamic values in their hearts. This is especially hard to do when you are raising a family in non-Muslim country embedded in a culture of disbelief. A lot of times the parents enrol their kids in Islamic school when younger or pay a teacher to teach them how to read Quran feeling that is effort will be enough to preserve their faith. It is not enough. Then later if and when that child is a teenager and gives up prayer or Islam altogether, the parents come crying to the imam hoping he is a miracle worker.

It takes more time than that. If one has the options and financial opportunities available, one of the best thing parents can do is relocate to a place where Muslims are strong and family-focused and to provide your kids with such circles that provide ample opportunities to befriend righteous friends and have righteous role models. Sometimes Sufi orders or da'wah efforts like Tableeghi Jamaat or even Muslim Student Associations serve as great micro cultures to instil these positive values. And at the heart of it all is the family having a healthy connection to the masjid and having a healthy welcoming environment and a positive similar aged social circle there. If you feel healthy, welcoming, and positive social circles are not descriptors of your local masjid and the Muslim circles around, I suggest you more especially for your kids, or at the very least spend extra time to create an Allah-loving, Quran-loving, Prophet-loving, and Islam-loving environment in the home.

As Islam-loving and happy family, and Islam-loving set of friends, an Islam-loving community they feel they belong to, and an Islam-loving education and training are usually the ingredients that create star role model kids and role model Muslims.

PROTECTING OUR HOMES

> *"O you who have believed, protect yourselves and your own families from a Fire whose fuel is mankind and stones, (and) over which are harsh, severe Angels, who do not disobey Allah in whatever He commands them and who perform whatever they are commanded to."*

> (Q 66:6)

The Home is a blessing. The Prophet S advised us to keep to our homes during days of strife, confusion and fitnah.

In Surah Kahf we learn about the seven young men, who fled to the cave due to fear of harming their iman due to the immoralities of society. Allah made them sleep for 309 years as a protection for them.

Likewise, all the prophets sought refuge in caves at certain points in their lives. In the caves they would contemplate, reflect and seek nearness to Allah. Many awliyyah also used to flee to caves, because what can you do in a cave except worship Allah?

Today we also need to seek the caves to protect ourselves and our iman. But how to do that, when we live in cities nowhere near any caves? We have to build our own prophetic caves. These consist of:

- Attending majlis

- Sitting amongst the righteous

- Keeping good company of those who remind you of Allah

- Seeking knowledge

- Maintaining your modesty

If you build such a cave you will be protected and you will build up your iman. Allah will send the angels to accompany you. He will let blessings descend upon you.

May we all be protected from fitnah and be surrounded by good people and be blessed with yaqeen.

FAMILY

Even though our priority is our direct family (parents, siblings, spouse, kids, etc.) Allah wants us to maintain and keep a healthy relationship with the rest of our family as well. Even just the little stuff like talking, visiting, gift-giving, and expressing that your care makes a difference.

FRIENDS

Unlike family, for our spouse and our friends we have at least some choice. Just like for our children, I emphasized how key friends are to the growth of them or to their spiritual destruction. The same is true of us too. Good friends, especially those we can open up to about life's struggles and compete and work with in spiritual growth, are so influencing and empowering and can be the one key added element to our lives that give us eternal success. As for those in our social circles that still keep their evils and are pulling you down or rubbing off you must be kept a distance from as best as possible. This is why Ghazali temporarily and Fudail permanently moved out for they knew themselves and knew they would stay stuck in the same hypocrisy and spiritual emptiness if they stuck with the same location and same social circle of friends and associates.

BELIEVERS

Allah wants us to have good character with everybody in general, with special emphasis and the highest of dignity given to those who are a part of our Muslim ummah (nation). Allah does not look at those who have embraced the testimony of faith similarly as those who have not, we the people of faith are His chosen people.

Here then is an outline of some simple duties of brotherhood and sisterhood:

- To give greetings of salam to them
- To follow the funeral
- To visit the sick
- To accept their invitations

- To help those who are oppressed

- To fulfil the oaths

- To return the greetings

- To respond to the sneezer (saying Yarhamkumullah, Allah mercy on you, after the person who sneezed says Alhamdulillah. All praise and thanks be to Allah).

- To not harm with the hands or tongue unjustly

- To cover their faults

- To call towards good and call away from evil

- To not mock in person in person or speak ill of him behind his back

- To help them as best we can and at least pray for them when they are in distress.

- Along up all the after key character points mentioned throughout this book

Some other ideals we strive for:

- To love them for being carriers of La ilaha ilAllah and to love the righteous and lovers of Allah even more so in hopes you be like them and be of them in Qiyaamah.

- To prefer you brother's need over yourself

- To genuinely train and guide and empower those you can influence so you are a group of those who love each other for Allah's sake, the group of constant praisers of Allah that loves and that His angels frequent.

The Prophet ﷺ efforted and succeeded in uniting the two warring tribes of Madinah together all while they also embraced the emigrants from Makkah. Through His guidance and through the mercy of Allah, all the hearts were united and filled with deep love and brotherhood. The community was eventually blessed to share that love with each and the beautiful new faith they received from their Creator to the rest of Arabia and to the rest of the world.

NON-MUSLIMS

Our dealings with non-Muslims is just like with any other human being: to be done with respect and character. Just like the example of that Jewish boy that converted, the Prophet ﷺ worked with the hearts of the people and through the spiritual blessing of the Quran and his own deep relationship with Allah, eventually came to steal the hearts of the world, being the most beloved man to ever walk this earth. Teaching others of our faith is also essential in the hopes that to get illuminated with the truth or at the very least become more understanding of the teachings and of us as Muslims. There will always be enemies of Islam who harbor deep untannded hatred towards us and if we have to deal with such people we should do so with patience and wisdom, avoiding to lose our cool mindlessly or become reactionary and uncivilized. Patience and wisdom is the Prophet's ﷺ way.

THE NEEDY

Generosity is a virtue so highly emphasized by Allah and His Messenger ﷺ that if cannot be understated. You can see how generous a man is by how quickly he responds to taking care of the needs of strangers.

There is something especially heart-softening when you actually bring food and break bread with these hungry, for in that moment of sitting and eating together you realize that the poor are human being just like everyone else just stuck in the test of Allah of poverty for the time being. This makes one more grateful of what one has and more attuned to giving back.

The Prophet ﷺ whole life revolved around giving – giving guidance to the people to achieve eternal success, giving answers to the solutions of people's life issues they brought, and giving food and money and shelter to those in need of it as best he could. Make sure you are not only giving your minimum 2.5% of wealth for Zakah charity, but also making it a weekly habit in giving it. And take extra time out to feed the poor, visit the sick, attend to the funeral, and speak to those who are struggling in and need some encouraging words.

6.   CHASTITY

Chastity is the last beautiful quality of good character we will mention but definitely not the least important. Haya, which can be translated as modesty or bashfulness, is something the Prophet ﷺ praised and also defended when he saw the quality in others.

While clearing Aisha's (R) name of all the slander and false accusations, our final judge and Lord of all courts, broke his silence on how serious he takes adultery and lewd behavior.

> *"The woman and the man guilty of adultery or fornication – flog them each with 100 stripes. Let not compassion move you in their case, in a manner prescribed by Allah, if you believe Allah and the Last Day.*
>
> *And let a party witness their punishment. Let no man guilty of adultery or fornication marry any but a woman similarly guilty or a polytheist. Nor let any fornicator or*

adulterous woman marry adulterous man or a polytheist. Forbidden is the act for the true believer."

(Quran24: 3-4)

It is interesting how far many other forbidden things like alcohol or gambling, Allah kept silent at least within the Quran of any form of punishment. Yet adultery / fornication is such a cross of the line that right in the beginning does it specially the strict punishment for it – 100 stripes of the whip, that should be publicly. On top of that they shall be barred from the regular pure believer marriage circle. In most circumstances such severity in courts are not implemented as Allah later in the Surah requires 4 witnesses to testify to the crime which is hard to do. Nevertheless it shows the severity by which Allah sees it. Why is it so vile and filthy in Allah's eyes? One reason Allah calls for a way of life and society which honors to protect families and to create an environment that allows smoothly to create new families so the legacy of Islam continues generation to generation. But when zina becomes prevalent in a society, it leads to the destruction of the very fabric of the family and leads the people involved into so many other vices.

"And don't come near unlawful sex for it is a shameful deed and an evil path (to follow that leads to hardship and misery and other evils)."

(Quran 17:32)

America as well as, western society in the 20th century are perfect examples of the deterioration of society's morals as zina becomes more widespread. For in the early 1900's women were more well-dressed and family oriented with official laws if a woman's clothing was above her knees. As the evil liberation movement occurred now even wearing next to nothing is considered acceptable and just to fulfil their curiosity young men and women lose their virginity what has this let to culturally? It's led to a culture where any man and woman is seeking his or her own pleasure, where cheating is common and rampant along with divorces, where families are easily broken and where many broken-hearted kids are left abandoned and end up doing all sorts of crimes in the name of this search to find some "family" or gang to belong to.

It has led to a society that worships the body and worships sex, at the expense of destroying its relationship to the Creator and to disconnecting from the high values of the spiritual path.

So what does Islam recommend to honor the value of modesty? A few things.

First is honor and reflect on the blessings of family. A young man come to the Prophet ﷺ saying that he loved and could respect every tenet of Islam except for zina. The Prophet ﷺ reversed to a question that would make him understand. He ﷺ basically asked the young how he would feel if another man fulfilled such zina intentions on his mother or sister, on how he would feel about that. Anger and hate surged in the young man's blood. Of course he would be extremely angry at their family member and being the tribal Arab that he was, would seriously hurt the guy. The Prophet ﷺ then put his hand on the man's heart and prayed a special prayer for him. He said that he walked in there with zina being the most beloved thing in his heart and he walked out with zina being the most detested thing in his heart.

One great lesson we as men especially can get from this is that the spirit of protecting our women we love from haram's way is the spirit we need to carry to all women. How? By honoring their dignity and the institution of marriage and not falling to zina even with the woman or women that love us we preserve a culture of purity and chastity and family – togetherness. Ultimately we as men and women of Allah are preservers of Allah's culture of Quran and this culture of Islam by humbly honoring the laws that Allah has set down and loving the guidance and way of the true deen defenders on earth that Allah so dearly and so passionately loves and happily rewards with eternal treasures and a blissful abode and an eternally joyous life beyond our wildest dreams and imaginations and desires! May Allah make us those true deen defenders.

Secondly we should learn to lower our gaze from those tempting or forbidden to us for the more you let your eyes wander, the more you'll let your tongue wander, and the more at risk you'll be at letting your private part to wander in unlawful ways. He/she that only sees pure things and only holds that in his/her heart will speak purely and act purely.

> *"Say to the believing men that they should lower their gaze and guard their modesty – that is purer for them. Certainly Allah is well-informed of all that they do.*
>
> *And say to the believing women that they should lower their gaze and preserve their modesty and they should not display their beauty and ornaments except what (ordinarily) appear thereof and that they should draw veils over themselves and that they should not display their beauty except to their husbands, their fathers, their husbands' father, their sons, their husbands' sons, their brother or their brothers' sons, or their sisters' sons, or their women, or the one their right hand possesses, or male attendants free of desires or small children who do not yet have carnal desire. And also that they should not strike*

their feet in order to draw attention to their beauty. And oh believers! Turn you all together towards Allah in repentance so you may be successful!"

(Quran24: 30-31)

In these beautiful verses Allah is calling believing men and women to embrace the culture of modesty by lowering our gazes, dressing modestly, being socially aware of those socially around us, and not engaging in any seductive behaviors that lead to us or others falling into indecency. Although the word "khumur" is used instead of "hijab", it is through this verse and through the Prophet's ﷺ words we extract the command for women to cover their hair and their bodies out of modesty and dignity.

When a non-Muslim, especially a Christian, asks me about why many Muslims men have beards and many Muslims women cover their hair, I happily point back to the paintings of Jesus (AS), who had a beard, and Mary (AS), who dressed modestly and covered her hair. We simply put love the righteous and the chosen guides and follow their way, for they listened and obeyed and showed us the way.

For the single, beyond just reflecting on the blessing of family, marrying and starting one's family helps one settle down and protect oneself.

"Marry those among you who are single and the righteous male and female servants you have. If they are in poverty, Allah will provide means out of His grace, for Allah is ample-giving and knower of all things."

(Quran 24:32)

If one cannot yet get married or is waiting to get married but the desire for companionship is still too strong, the Prophet ﷺ recommended to fast as hunger weakens the bodily energies and helps calm the desires especially when it is coupled with spiritual practices such as quieting the mind or prayer that help us rewire our patterned ways of thinking. That, along with avoiding as best one can those tempting to us and those environments inducing us (like simple public places, events, or every other haram places like clubs) shall help us in the journey of us overcoming our base desires and completely giving ourselves to Allah, making His service and pleasure alone the purpose of our lives.

A deep spiritual practice helps us in illuminating our hearts, eyes and our very eyes in seeing the light of Allah and in perceiving His very presence around us. Having a good connection to the masjid and a spiritual circle around us helps us ground ourselves in grounding us in the values we strive to live by.

In interacting with the opposite gender that is marriageable to us, the Prophet ﷺ guided us to not losing interact with them or attend to mixed gatherings, but rather to maintain interactions with respect and in a public setting and in a professional and polite manner. This in no way means that Islam calls for women to stay away from the public affairs of society, for Khadijah (R) was the Prophet's ﷺ wife who was a successful businesswomen, Aisha (R) became a world-renown teacher and scholar of Islam teaching men and women, Zaynab, the Prophet's ﷺ daughter, publicly addressed the community when a personal issued happened, Nusaybah (R) was praised by the Prophet ﷺ for engaging in battle defending the Prophet ﷺ as the enemy army encroached on him, the

Prophet ﷺ encouraged all the women in their household to keep giving in charity and giving back to the community, and the wife of Umar (R) would happily go to the masjid even though he didn't like it too much for that was one of her rights both of them understood to her having. In Makkah, the women were more humble and obedient and the society more masculine-dominated, whereas in Madinah the women were more vocal and active and in both the Prophet ﷺ laid down the essential principles and values to live and operate by. The culture were respected as long as they didn't conflict with Allah's laws or principles in which case it was cleansed and purified to be an Allah-pleasing culture. And that is part of the versatility and beauty of Islam, the anchor is one and the same which is our connection to Allah and His words and His Prophet (S), yet the expression in cultures take variety of forms and has throughout the centuries.

CONCLUSION

Alhamdulillah we have covered a lot of ground on summarizing the essentials of the Islamic spiritual path, discussing the realization of tawheed, the embodiment of taqwa and reverential Allah-conscious righteousness, and expressing true Islamic and beautiful akhlaaq and character with others. There's so much more we could have included, or expanded on further, but no doubt this was a very thorough and illuminating overview.

The goal of this section so far has been to establish those spiritual ideals we have and to give you a simple yet effective framework for you to use at any time to check and see where you are in life, self-accountability and self-awareness are essential mental skills to develop that are keys to the paths. Reading the sections, you can ask, "How focused was in my prayers?" or "How much in awe am I when reading Allah's words?" or "How much love to others have I expressed?" and similar questions that help you focus on developing yourself and to improved your relationship with Allah, yourself, others, and the world.

Balance is also essential in the path. Just as the Prophet ﷺ motivated his people to do more acts of righteousness, he similarly warned them against extremism in religion. When some young companion figured that they were more sinful than the Prophet ﷺ and thus had to do more good, to the point where they suggested to fast every day, to pray all night, without sleep, and to not get married the Prophet ﷺ corrected them and told them to follow his lifestyle and way, to fast some days and leave others, to pray good part of the night but also give yourself healthy sleep, and to get married. Too many people go too fast in the path without guidance and thus fall flat faced eventually. When it was told that the Prophet's ﷺ own daughter would pray so much at night in the masjid that she tied a rope behind her to support herself when exhausted from standing, the Prophet ﷺ corrected her by having no belt and letting the extra prayer finish by that point so you can get some sleep. To the famously righteous and completely detached to this world companion Abu Dharr, the Prophet ﷺ reminded him too that just as Allah had rights that he (R) was so thoroughly fulfilling so too does his body also have rights along with his wife and the people around him who also have rights over him. The Prophet ﷺ was the most closest to Allah and he showed us how to be extremely pure and righteous yet extremely balanced at the same time. What a beautiful heart and character he had (S)! Allah make us follow his ﷺ way.

Lastly, if there is only one lesson you got from all this section then let it be this: who you hang around and allow to influence you can either make you or break you. One good friend or companion or can alone be the reason by the love and influence on you of which can grant you to paradise. And one bad friend or companion or teacher can alone be the reason by the love and influence on you of which can get you a one-way ticket to the Hell-fire. On the Day of Judgement there will be no blaming another for our failings. We must be responsible in deciding who we interacted with. So who do you interact with daily? How do they influence you? Who do you need to be hanging out with?

May Allah grant you and me and all of us an empowering social circle and great success on the spiritual path and eternal success in the afterlife.

SECTION 3:

THE MISSION

HAVING TRUE "FIKR" FOR THE DEEN!

The war was bloody. The Muslims were losing. There was a mess. The nonbelievers were happy. They'd encircled the Prophet ﷺ. And in the midst of the dust-ridden battleground, cries shouted. "The Prophet is dead!," they exclaimed. All the remaining battle spirit of the companions was now lost. What's the point in fighting if the Prophet himself had passed.

It was in that heat of a moment, that the valiant hero Anas bin Nadr stood forward. He screamed, "if the Messenger of Allah has passed, then die as he died and fight!!"

"O Allah! I apologize to You for what these (i.e. his companions) have done, and I denounce what these (i.e. the pagans) have done." Then he advanced and Sa`ad bin Mu`adh met him. He said, "O Sa`d bin Mu`adh ! By the Lord of An-Nadr, Paradise! I am smelling its aroma coming from before (the mountain of) Uhud!"

He ran into the battlefield and fought without any fear of death. He put terror in the heart of his enemies. Even with multiple wounds all over his body gushing forth, he kept fighting till he was surrounded and stabbed the final blow. His body was found with more than eighty wounds of swords and arrows. Only his sister could recognize his body by his fingers.

Later it was found out the Prophet had not died, and that it had only been a rumor spread in the community to make the believers lose morale. Yet Anas found his victory that day. Anas was accepted by Allah and attained the station of Paradise! Later on Sa`d said, "O Allah's Apostle! I cannot achieve or do what he (i.e. Anas bin An-Nadr) did."

The Sahabah would say that the following verse of Quran was revealed concerning him and other men of his sort:

> "Among them is he who has fulfilled his vow [to the death], and among them is he who awaits [his chance]. And they did not alter [the terms of their commitment] by any alteration".

(Quran, 33:23)

The Prophet ﷺ was totally dedicated and gave his life to his Allah-given duty to live the message, deliver the message, and establish a community (known in Arabic, as "ummah") that revolves around the message. And the companions like Anas bin Nadr around him followed and did the same.

In the minds and hearts of the companions, the Messenger of Allah had instilled a spirit of giving their whole lives for the sake of Islam. This concern, or "fikr" in Arabic, was an obsession and a passion for them. They wanted to please their Lord and were willing to do whatever it took to get there.

Beyond believing fully in the message and living it as best they could, they gave their houses, their wealth, their time, their energy, and in certain cases like above their lives for the sake of Islam's protection and spreading. They took the Prophetic mission as their own mission just as they were instructed.

The Companions and true Muslim realize that now, with the sad reality of the Prophet S not being physically present with us, that the doors of revelation are closed. CLOSED. What has been revealed is final. And that it is our turn to spread this message.

Amongst those who come to the noble path of Islam, many keep their Islam to themselves. They pray, they fast, they are kind to others, but that's it. They don't think or worry or work towards supporting the Muslim community in other ways; it is not part of their DNA yet.

Indeed the spirit of this book comes from a spirit of having fikr of the deen. And we hope that not only does one get inspired to believe in the beauty of the revelation and to embrace its noble path of righteousness but also that our readers rekindle their minds and hearts to give their lives in the cause of supporting Allah's deen and chosen way of life of Islam in whatever way they can.

ISLAM & THE HISTORIC BATTLE FOR TRUTH

In these times of great opportunity and great struggle, we as the community of Believers and the carriers of the final revelation of Allah, must unite together and work hard and diligently against the onslaught of evil. We must not lose hope, for we as a community have faced worse and came back on top. We must not lose sight of the goal for we have our Lord Most High that we soon shall meet. Whereas previous chapters set the Quranic ideals for our character development, this section deals with activism and the necessity to move forward as a community in all domains of human endeavours.

Nations have come and gone in the struggle. Noah (AS) came to invite his people to the right way, yet only those few that accepted were saved, and the rest and the majority unfortunately denied his message and continued to be polytheistic and were drowned in the Great flood. Moses to the Egyptians, Jesus to the Jews, Salih was sent to the people of Thamud, Hud to the people of A'ad, Lot to the people of Sodom and Gomorrah, etc. Most humans continued the similar tragic pattern of denying the messenger and the simple message of beauty and love and oneness of God and obeying Him that he was calling them towards. They instead started challenging or hurting him and then eventually were destroyed.

Then came our Prophet ﷺ. He came with the message and through Allah's help established a community that spans from Africa all the way to China. But the work is not done. The mission continues to invite others and to organize ourselves in the best way we can. It is our job to effort in whatever way we can to serve others with the most noble of character and love and kindness and also in especially serving them by the inviting them with love and wisdom to the path of Islam.

The vision of changing the ummah!

We all need a vision sometimes to inspire us to work at higher levels. Here's something I wrote years back for an organization I was a part of which is not in operation anymore. We invited people to a three part process of discovering, joining and learning, then leading. We also wrote this beautiful vision which I hope inspires you as it did us:

Allah says:

YOU ARE indeed the best community that has ever been brought forth for [the good of] mankind: you enjoin the doing of what is right and forbid the doing of what is wrong, and you believe in Allah.

(3:110)

The vision of our Da'wah Mission is to become the largest and most influential group of Muslims in the history of the Ummat Muhammad, salAllahu a'laihi wasalam. To spread the banner of laa ilaha illAllah, not by reactionary pleas and revolts, but by the most effective means possible. We envision this group to be the pride of the ummah, the one that everyone desires to join. We intend to create a community making the average bored Muslim youth be inspired and dedicated to serve the ummah, and grow up to another level where it supports a whole community of true students of knowledge, saints and social workers, visionaries and global-influencing leaders, who are humble yet confident!

We will create a generation and a community of youth who are the future movers and shakers of the Ummah, who are brilliant students of knowledge, with variety of skills, balanced in their life, visionaries, supportive of one another, leaders of the righteous! They will bring not only their communities, but will raise the whole world to new heights. History will look back on our pioneering work as being the driving force that awakened the Ummah giant!

3 parts:

> 1)   Training and teaching the da'ees not only how to do da'wah but also u'loom of the deen

> 2)   Making these trained da'ees blossom into leaders in their own fields and able to spread the message and influences to the MASSES all over the world!

> 3) And ultimately our vision of the ummah is to see it on top. To be the spiritual and economic and political powerhouse of the world!

Our nabiyy Muhammad has left us with the complete book, the complete sunnah, and the complete deen, and We are inheriting and representing Him by doing the job of the prophets!

Just imagine yourself in front of Allah and you are like the man from out of town who did da'wah mentioned in Surah yaseen!

After all his efforts, Allah says to him after his passing:

> "It was said to him: 'Enter Paradise.' He said: "Woe to me!! Would that my people knew! "That my Lord (Allâh) has forgiven me, and made me of the honoured ones!"

May Allah grant us the same good fortune!

Our **Purpose** is to provide a platform and resources and guidance for our members to contribute to the greater purpose of benefiting the ummah!

Our **Focus** is to change the condition of the Muslim ummah starting locally then working towards globally!

Our **Standard** is that with each project we work on, our followers will have their lives effected more in the few days with our services than they have ever before!

Our **Work Ethic** is to demand more from our group members, volunteers, and staff than anyone else would because we are working for the sake of pleasing Allah.

Our **Method** is to teach Islam and imbibe powerful life skills in our team in a manner that is easily digestible and entertaining, while never sacrificing quality and depth. By these means, we will cherish the teamwork they build, the friendships we make, the knowledge we attain, the actions we strive to to do, and the eagerness we gain to support and the Ummah!

Ultimately, our purpose is to make Muslims GIANTS in respect to their knowledge, eman, righteousness as a collective community! Working together towards the same goal of seeking Allah's pleasure and getting Jannah! The purpose is to bring all of humanity closer to Allah, and equip the Muslims to service their communities and humanity at large!

We're here to change the course of humanity! Write our part of history! Seek Allah's pleasure in the most best of ways for Allah deserves no less than the best!

And there is no success except with Allâh, In Him do I place my complete trust and to Him I humbly return & repent!

(Surah Hud: 88)

3 AREAS OF SKILLS TO DEVELOP:

1. Thinking and information management Skills

The upcoming star missionary must be ready to learn how to think. This includes learning the rules of logic, language, and sharpening thinking and writing skills.

Information management is also essential. We are bombarded with so much information that we in general live with the overload as a default. By learning to organize information and reference it properly at the right time, we can be more successful in all areas of life.

2. Personal Organization and Internal and External Empowerment

Mental toughness

Ability to effectively organize one's self

3. Relationship Skills

Ability to effectively lead and organize others towards powerful goals This includes leadership, communication, and conflict resolution.

ESSENTIAL COMMUNITY FOCUSES

Any community work must start with a spirit of gratitude for where we are at Allah has blessed us with a blessed global community and blessed us with the Quran and with a spiritual tradition that is well and alive to this day. Alhamdulillah, all praise and thanks are to Allah! Here then are some of the essential community focuses we need to have in order to progress faster in the direction of our noble destiny.

1)   KINDNESS, RIGHTEOUSNESS, AND CHARITY

We have talked in detail about developing good character and righteousness in the previous section. Too many people get too busy in changing the world, that they forget to be kind to their parents, siblings, spouse, or children. Too many people are so obsessed with the problems of the world yet they themselves can't even wake up for their morning prayer or break their own personal addictions that Allah is displeased with.

It goes without saying that having maintaining the rules and guidelines that Allah has set as well as having a selfless spirit in serving Allah and His creation is necessary for any aspirant who wishes to contribute to global change and in serving the ummah.Never compromise on your character and kindness and love towards others, especially your nearest ones at home and those in your community, in the process of trying to make other big changes happen.

On a bigger level, the world is filled with so much suffering, poverty, war, and pain, so more effort is needed in the humanitarian efforts. However much is going on is not enough. We need more love to spread and for hate spread in the name of difference of country, race, religion, creed to be overcome.

2)   EDUCATION

It is a tragedy of how low the standards of education and character development are in many Muslim countries. This has to change. We need people who work together to reform the education system in ways where the tradition and the scripture can speak more with the natural and humanistic sciences being studies. Those intending to lead or be a part of such reform need to also study the philosophy of science and of education to be better informed about the background premises in the system that need changing.

Character building, emotional and social intelligence, and a deep faith and practice in Islam are things that must be powerfully integrated within our school systems so that we raise generation of righteous and beautifully-charactered individuals. The majority of higher learning institutions and the greatest of thinkers and minds are from outside Muslim lands. At one point in history the opposite was true. Only by first "catching up" and then innovating can we be a part of and influencing agent in the global conversations of academics and of spiritual and personal development.

3)   SPIRITUAL CIRCLES

We need to support those leading spiritual and personal day circles and need to spread moral of such circles. These could be those circles led to a traditional Sufi manner with the master and the many disciples all seeking deeper being and refined character and can also be those who are now sprouting and using science and mindfulness based and psychology-backed approaches to personal development that is still in line with the Quran and Sunnah.

Sufism in today's day has gotten a mixed reputation amongst some Muslim communities with some hating it direly. This is because some have posed under the guise as a "sufi" and then used their relationship as a spiritual mentor to steal money, abuse others, and make them do funky mindless practices. Worse, some of these fake gurus call towards a level of worship of graves and themselves, have introduced intoxicants and dancing to their circles, have stated they are not in need of praying the Salah prayers or following the commandments of Allah as they are "above" such limitations, and have established their circles in a completely cult-like in fashion using the word "sufi" as a cover up for their inner evil. But this is not what real Sufism is nor should all of sufism be judged to be bad because of such individuals. In general though, the real Sufism is focused on us mastering the inner dimension of commands of our deen like pure dhikr, pure prayer, pure following of the Quran and sunnah, learning how to live with "ihsaan," excellence, "taqwa," Allah-consciousness, "khushoo'," fearful awe of Allah, amongst many other great qualities (as we have discussed in our "those immersed in beauty" section). And real sufism has been a positive in our history, with great minds like Shaykh Ibn Taymiyyah and Ibn Qayyim and Imam Nawawi and Shaykh Suyuti all supporting or sitting in the tutelage of the real men of this science who called towards inner purification and beauty so we are ready to present ourselves before Allah.

4) MISSIONARY WORK

The Muslims of the first generation were passionate to call others to Islam. They preached and called others towards the beauty of this faith. You find graves of the companions of the Prophet ﷺ as far as China, Turkey, and Morocco. They were evangelical with their Islam and felt blessed and responsible to spread it as best they could. And they did. Now it's our turn and we must do the same and be willing to take the time, energy, organization, strategization, and collective effort necessary to spread Islam.

5)   COMPUTERS, TECHNOLOGY, AND INNOVATION

Computers and technology have disrupted history and changed the way we fundamentally live and how we connect to one another. Communication, education, banking, media, politics, what hasn't been altered by technology! We need more minds and the brightest of minds to be at the frontier of the innovation.

One of the current advantages of the technology world is that the playing field is levelled and even poorer countries can more easily create softwares and other technologies that compete with even stronger brands but are much better financed. Another great field emerging is what is called social entrepreneurship where entrepreneurs and businessmen especially in the world of technology create businesses that are not only profitable but are also helping solve global problems like poverty, environmental destruction, abuse of women and the weak, etc. The possibilities are endless for the people that are dedicated!

6)   BANKING, INVESTMENTS, AND DEVELOPMENT

Many people are obsessed by what they call the "New World Order", connecting many families and secret societies to the power structures that contract the world. Whenever such conversation is obsessed over, we must always step back and appreciate the "Ultimate World Order, that Allah always was and always is the one who holds all power and directs and controls man's affair. Only after a deep realization and acceptance of that should we go into our studies of the power dynamics of the world. Usually if you follow the money underneath the surface you can see who's really in power.

The quest for wealth has dominated the world of politics and wealthier nations use their wealth to keep weaker nation in poverty so they can more easily control them and can easily take advantage of their resources for their own benefit. Banks of these wealthier nations are at the heart of the political game: the weaker countries need money to survive and to develop their country and so they'll almost be forced to take these foreign loans, many of which are impossible to pay off their current revenues especially with the compounded interest on them. As communities and countries of Muslims become wealthier, it's important for us not only to learn the ropes enough to start our own banks along with Shariah-compliant loans, but also to sit down and come up with creative banking solutions that help alleviate social problems and empower weaker and poorer peoples with the opportunity to make a better life for themselves. Faith-inspired international collaboration and development!

7) POLITICS OF UNITY

We cannot survive in a world that is constantly fighting with one another, man has successfully created such weapons that can annihilate the whole human population if used against one another. What makes the matter worse is that in such times where great leadership is necessary to be seen, we have Muslims spending their time fighting and even going to war with other Muslims and that too for the pettiest of tribalistic and nationalistic of reasons. How can a nation that Allah intended to be as guides and models for other nations ever fulfil that role if we are too busy bickering with one another and pulling each others legs down? This of course isn't true of all Muslim countries, but it is true of many.

How do we reverse the trend and bring about more unity and cooperation? This positive spirit and the sense of togetherness comes from people and a shift in attitudes of people, and that shift can only come through education, grassroots movements, and with strong leadership that puts that shift in attitude and in policy as a high priority goal. Leader like historic figures like Salahuddin Ayubi need to be created and developed. It is at this point we will say that politics of unity also means to gain strength in every field as well: to have a strong military, banking system, currency, culture, economy, and transparent and integrity in leadership and in the masses all helps then bring us more towards the goal of achieving peace and unity. If the goal is power and expressing authority itself, the efforts will be without blessing, but if the goal is pleasing Allah and bringing the best for people, then our efforts will be focused and blessed.

A big part of the unifying will happen when we learn to tolerate one another and appreciate the differences of one another. There are too many politically charged overzealous and radical Muslim groups that are nitpicking minor differences and are ready to bear arms and kill others. This is radicalization at its extreme and it is a cancer we as a community have to free ourselves from. The Prophet ﷺ warned us of such extremism in the religion, and he warned his community that in the future will come people that will pray and fast more than usual but will quickly commit Kufr, or acts of disbelief that take you out of the folds. Part of this deradicalization can only happen if we as a mass of Muslims academically look at the traditions within the Quran and hadeeth with a new light and a healthy open mind to find greater depth and new meaning in it while honoring the natural sciences in a way that effectively communicates to us in the modern world we live in. The task is great, the conversation has started with men like Jamal Al-Afghani and Muhammad Iqbal, and the potential for great minds to achieve this task are also there, but the push is needed to further this work en masse. In the end of the day, we must hope and pray for the best, prepare for the worst, and always do our part to furthering ourselves and our community in the right direction.

8)   MEDIA AND CULTURE

They who control the media control the minds and hearts of the people. We as a community need to have healthy sources of news, avoiding news and media outlets that are just portraying lies of the global powers that be and demonizing the Muslims. We need outlets of media and entertainment and cultural expressions that are faith-based, that strive for integrity and a global outlook, and that inspire people positively with a spirit of open-mindedness, contribution, and a diversity of thinking presented.

We have mentioned how honoring and keeping alive our own Muslim cultures is important, whether that be the clothing, cooking, arts ,or architecture of a place, but at the same time we need another group of people within the community who involve themselves in the different circles of global and popular culture, cautiously approaching it and ensuring not to partake in the activities within it that are displeasing to Allah, while still immersing oneself in it to bring good from it and guide the people who are leading it to good. We need to celebrate our artists, writers, poets, architects, historians, and story-tellers!

We need greater Muslim representation in these fields so we have influence and authority to represent the positive and beautiful deen that Islam is and to combat the negative portrayals and labels that many news and media outlets and even cultural icons and movies and books and world leaders still perpetuate. We need our own books and movies and news organizations and media outlets and cultural icons that break the cycle and give us our voice back. If we're not on the table then we may find ourselves on the menu!

9)   EMPOWERMENT AND ORGANIZATION

Our education, our communities, our interactions need to be empowering to others. Financially, spiritually, physically, and socially empowering people to be better people and better versions of themselves and to discover the Lord Most High whose and awareness is present throughout all of existence, ready to illuminate any one of us that are willing to turn to Him.

A lot of times, community organizers are well-intentioned but not rounded enough spiritually to have real impact, or have big dreams but do not create the right team and organization necessary to make the difference they so desire.

Self-empowering ourselves means to stop the cycle of blaming and hating others for our problems. It means for us to take full responsibility for our actions anad take full responsibility for bettering our circumstances. The Quran was and is not only a Book that honors the eternal truth and correct history of what happened in the past, but was a guide that drove the Muslim community to its own great heights of worldly success and it can be that for us today too if we let it and embrace its spirit and message.

The Quran was Allah guiding them to individual moral and spiritual excellences while also guiding their organization and communal development. The examples of this are numerous.

For example, after the first major battle of the Muslims at Badr, Allah revealed verses about his divine support on that day and helped them put their victory in context:

"If anything that is good befalls you, it grieves them; but if some misfortune overtakes you, they rejoice at it. But if you are constant and do right, not the least harm will their cunning do to you; for Allah Encompasses round about all that they do.

Remember that morning you did leave your household (early) to post the faithful at their stations for battle: And Allah hears and knows all things:

Remember two of your parties Meditated cowardice; but Allah was their protector, and in Allah should the faithful (Ever) put their trust.

Allah had helped you at Badr, when you were a contemptible little force; then fear Allah. thus May you show your gratitude.

Remember you said to the Faithful: "Is it not enough for you that Allah should help you with three thousand angels (especially) sent down?

"Yes, - if you remain firm, and act aright, even if the enemy should rush here on you in hot haste, your Lord would help you with five thousand angels Making an onslaught.

Allah made it but a message of hope for you, and an assurance to your hearts: (in any case) there is no help except from Allah, The Exalted, the Wise!

(Quran 3:120-126)

When the Prophet S signed the treaty of Hudaibiyah for peace between the Muslims and the pagan Meccans, and did so with terms that favored the Meccans and thus frustrated the Muslims who were tired of being taken advantage of, Allah revealed verses that shifted their whole perspective of the situation: celebrate and rejoice for although you may not see it, this treaty is a great victory and a blessing from the Divine Himself:

"Verily We have granted you a manifest Victory: That Allah may forgive you thy faults of the past and those to follow; fulfil His favour to you; and guide you on the Straight Way; And that Allah may help you all with powerful support. It is He Who sent down tranquillity into the hearts of the Believers, that they may add faith to their faith;- for to Allah belong the Forces of the heavens and the earth; and Allah is Full of Knowledge and Wisdom;-

That He may admit the men and women who believe, to Gardens beneath which rivers flow, to dwell therein for aye, and remove their ills from them;- and that is, in the sight of Allah, the highest achievement (for man),-And that He may punish the Hypocrites, men and women, and the Polytheists men and women, who imagine an evil opinion of Allah. On them is a round of Evil: the Wrath of Allah is on them: He has cursed them and got Hell ready for them: and evil is it for a destination.

For to Allah belong the Forces of the heavens and the earth; and Allah is Exalted in Power, Full of Wisdom. We have truly sent you as a witness, as a bringer of Glad Tidings, and as a Warner: In order that you (O men) may believe in Allah and His Messenger, that you may assist and honour Him, and celebrate His praise morning and evening.

> *Verily those who plight their fealty to you do no less than plight their fealty to Allah. the Hand of Allah is over their hands: then any one who violates his oath, does so to the harm of his own soul, and any one who fulfils what he has covenanted with Allah,- Allah will soon grant him a great Reward.*

(Quran 48:1-10)

And even when the Muslim community transitioned from a local movement to a national one with tribes upon tribes embracing Islam throughout the peninsula, Allah revealed these words:

> *"When comes the Help of Allah, and Victory, And you dost see the people enter Allah's Religion in crowds, Celebrate the praises of thy Lord, and pray for His Forgiveness: For He is Oft-Returning (in Grace and Mercy)."*

(Quran 110:1-3)

From the beginning to the end of the Prophet's S life, Allah was there the whole time. And from the beginning till the end of our Muslim community's presence on this earth, Allah was there and is there all the time. We as a community face many intellectual, spiritual, and social challenges, and yet we shall not give up hope for we have a history, a community, and an identity. Our predecessors have faced and overcame even greater challenges in the past so we could continue the legacy and be blessed with the deen of Islam, and so we too must strive and overcome.

Let us organize ourselves, working the system intelligently instead of being worked by it, let us grow ourxx selves to greater and greater heights!

KEEPING IT REAL

Now it's Your Turn:

1. Go find educational videos or books on Muslim heroes or on Islamic history (videos are all over the internet, books like (like Destiny Disrupted or Venture of Islam or a biographical works) so you know more about your past.

2. Find your special talent and gift, hone and give back to your community and ummah. Start with giving at least one hour this week.

3. Make a list of three inspiring people in your preferred field that is making a difference in the world.

Reflection Questions:

1. Where are places in your life or in your career where you can contribute more towards serving others?

2. What people or groups can you join hands with to contribute more towards serving others?

3. Where is history going and where is the future of the ummah?

CONCLUSION

This work has been a labor of love for the Book that has inspired and reformed millions throughout the ages including myself. It is the perfect revelation, unaltered, and heavenly sent as a mercy to those who follow it.

We have explored many unique passages of the Quran, including the lives of the Messenger of Allah S, Musa AS, Jesus AS, and the spirituality, the individual practice and the community that the Quran and that Islam calls for. Even so, we have only touched the tip of the iceburg of the noble world that is the Quran. More than just a summary of the Quran, which in actuality is impossible to truly do, I hope that this work ignited and fueled a new love for you with the Quran and deepened your relationship with it. I hope it inspired you to take your life more seriously and to live it more faithfully in preparation of the Great Day where we are either sentenced to the Fire or honored with entry to the delightful Gardens! I hope it inspired you to a new level of respect for your fellow righteous Muslims who are part of the beautiful story of the Quran manifesting its light in the world.

Let this not be the end of the journey but rather the beginning.

Let us end first with prayers from the Sacred Book and from the Walking Quran S himself:

All the Praises are for You: You are the Lord of the Heavens and the Earth. All the Praises are for You; You are the Maintainer of the Heaven and the Earth and whatever is in them. All the Praises are for You; You are the Light of the Heavens and the Earth. Your Word is the Truth, and Your Promise is the Truth, and the Meeting with You is the Truth, and Paradise is the Truth, and the (Hell) Fire is the Truth, and the Hour is the Truth. O Allah! I surrender myself to You, and I believe in You and I depend upon You, and I repent to You and with You (Your evidences) I stand against my opponents, and to you I leave the judgment (for those who refuse my message). O Allah! Forgive me my sins that I did in the past or will do in the future, and also the sins I did in secret or in public. You are my only God (Whom I worship) and there is no other God for me (i.e. I worship none but You)." [Sahih al-Bukhari 7385]

> "O Allah, by Your knowledge of the unseen and Your power over creation, keep me alive so long as You know that living is good for me and cause me to die when You know that death is better for me. O Allah, cause me to fear You in secret and in public. I ask You to make me true in speech in times of pleasure and of anger. I ask You to make me moderate in times of wealth and poverty. And I ask You for everlasting delight and joy that will never cease. I

ask You to make me pleased with that which You have decreed and for an easy life after death. I ask You for the sweetness of looking upon Your face and a longing to meet You in a manner that does not entail a calamity that will bring about harm or a trial that will cause deviation. O Allah, beautify us with the adornment of faith and make us among those who guide and are rightly guided."

[Sunan an-Nasa'i 1305]

"The Messenger believes in what hath been revealed to him from his Lord, as do the men of faith. Each one (of them) believes in Allah, His angels, His books, and His apostles. "We make no distinction (they say) between one and another of His apostles." And they say: "We hear, and we obey: (We seek) Your forgiveness, our Lord, and to you is the end of all journeys."

On no soul doth Allah Place a burden greater than it can bear. It gets every good that it earns, and it suffers every ill that it earns. (Pray:) "Our Lord! Condemn us not if we forget or fall into error; our Lord! Lay not on us a burden Like that which you didst lay on those before us; Our Lord! Lay not on us a burden greater than we have strength to bear. Blot out our sins, and grant us forgiveness. Have mercy on us. you art our Protector; Help us against those who stand against faith."

(Quran 2:285-286)

Oh Allah I surrender myself to you, I entrust my affairs to You, I turn my face to You, and lay myself down relying totally on You, putting my hopes on You and fearing You. There is no refuge and no escape with You. I believe in the

Book you have revealed and the Prophet whom you have sent.

(Muslim 2710)

"O Allah, I am Your slave, son of Your male servant, and son of Your female servant. My forelock is in Your Hand. Your command for me prevails. Your judgement concerning me is just. I beseech You through every name You have, including those you have named Yourself, including that You have taught to anyone in Your creation, including those of your names that You have mentioned in Your Book, or that You have kept unknown that you make the Qur'an be Springtime of my heart, the light of my chest, the remover of my sadness and the pacifier of my worries."

(Musnad Ahmad 1/391)

O Allah, have mercy on me by abandonment of sins forever, so long as You keep me remaining. And have mercy on me from taking upon myself what does not concern me, and provide me good sight for what will make You pleased with me. O Allah, Originator of the heavens and the earth, Possessor of glory, and generosity, and honor that is not exceeded. I ask you, O Allah, O Rahman, by Your glory and the light of Your Face, to make my heart constant in remembering Your Book as You taught me, and grant me that I recite it in the manner that will make You pleased with me. O Allah, Originator of the heavens and the earth, Possessor of glory, and generosity, and honor that is not exceeded. I ask you, O Allah, O Rahman, by Your glory and the light of Your Face, to enlighten my sight with Your Book, and make my tongue free with it, and to relieve my heart with it, and to expand my chest with it, and to wash my body with it. For indeed, none aids me upon the truth other than You, and none gives it except You, and there is no might or power except by Allah, the High, the Magnificent.

(Tirmidhi 3570)

"Our Lord! Accept from us this (service); verily You alone are the All-Hearing, the All-Knowing."

(Q 2: 127)